John Wenham

EASTER ENIGMA

John Wenham

Academie Books Grand Rapids, Michigan
Zondervan Publishing House

EASTER ENIGMA: ARE THE RESURRECTION ACCOUNTS IN CONFLICT?
Copyright © 1984 by John Wenham

Published by special arrangement with The Paternoster Press, Exeter, Devon, Great Britain.

ACADEMIE BOOKS is an imprint of Zondervan Publishing House, 1415 Lake Drive, S.E., Grand Rapids, Michigan 49506

Library of Congress Cataloging in Publication Data

Wenham, John
    Easter enigma.

    Includes bibliographical references and index.
      1. Jesus Christ—Resurrection—Biblical teaching.
2. Bible.   N.T.—Criticism, interpretation, etc.
I. Title.
BT481.W44   1984   232.9'7   84-5110
ISBN 0-310-29861-X

Printed in the United States of America

84 85 86 87 88 89 90 91 / 10 9 8 7 6 5 4 3 2 1

To
DAVID

Contents

Tables and Diagrams

Author's Thanks

I wish to express my warm thanks to the many friends who over the years have helped me in the preparation of this book. In particular to Roger Beckwith, Martin Brett, David Deboys, Mary Hayter, Geoffrey Holister, Ralph Houghton, Robin Leaver, Alec Maclehose, Tom Wright and my sons Gordon and David, who at various stages read the manuscript and made helpful comments; to Mary Long and Betty Ho Sang for their typing; and above all to Dennis Tarrant for doing the maps.

JOHN WENHAM

INTRODUCTION

An Intriguing Puzzle

"This Jesus God raised up, and of that we are witnesses," said Peter on the day of Pentecost. And from that day to this the resurrection of Jesus has been the spearhead of the Christian case. From it flows belief in the deity of Christ and all the other Christian truths. It is thus of first importance to know the value of the testimony of the New Testament witnesses. It is not of course essential to belief in the resurrection that the witnesses be faultless, but the whole case is gravely impaired if they can be shown to be seriously unreliable.

Now it so happens that the story of Jesus' resurrection is told by five different writers, whose accounts differ from each other to an astonishing degree. So much so that distinguished scholars one after another have said categorically that the five accounts are irreconcilable. Going back to the last century, the great radical, P.W. Schmiedel, said: "The Gospels ... exhibit contradictions of the most glaring kind. Reimarus ... enumerated ten contradictions; but in reality their number is much greater." Even the doughty conservative, Henry Alford, wrote: "Of all harmonies, those of the incidents of these chapters are to me the most unsatisfactory ... they seem to me to weaken instead of strengthening the evidence ... I have abandoned all idea of harmonizing throughout."

Coming to this century, P. Gardner-Smith says: "No ingenuity can make the narration of Luke consistent with that of Mark, much less is it possible to reconcile the picture presented by the fourth evangelist with the accounts of any of the synoptic writers. Mutually contradictory narratives cannot all be true ... Nothing can be made of a jumble of contradicting statements." E. Brunner says: "The sources contradict one another, and only a 'harmonizing' process which is not too much concerned about truth, could patch up a fairly connected account of the events, in which it is only too manifest that the later and less credible witnesses appear more important than the earlier, and more reliable ones. Such a dishonest way of dealing with the subject really has nothing to do with 'faith in the Word of God'; it only serves to support the disastrous prejudice that Christian faith is only possible in connexion with historical dishonesty." A.M. Ramsey, a relatively conservative writer, says: "It is a fascinating study to attempt to harmonize what the evangelists tell ... Up to a point the attempt may be successful, but a limit to the success is always reached." "That we should expect to be able to weave the stories into a chronological and geographical plan seems inconceivable."

With more recent writers the verdict is the same. P. Benoit (1969): "I think we have to give up any idea of reconciling John and the synoptics." C.F. Evans (1970) speaks of "the impression that it is not simply difficult to harmonize these traditions, but quite impossible." W. Marxsen (1970): "These stories cannot be harmonized." N. Perrin (1977) speaks of "glaring discrepancies." J.K. Elliott (1979) says "it is obvious that we cannot reconcile the accounts." I.H. Marshall (1977), however, speaks more cautiously (and challengingly?): "This is not to say that the narratives are necessarily irreconcilable, but that so far nobody has produced a convincing hypothesis."[1]

I first became interested in the subject in 1945 when living in Jerusalem not far from the old walled city. I got to know the sites in and around the city intimately. I had no real doubts that the gospel writers were honest and well informed people, providentially equipped by God to give the church a sound account of these events, but I was by no means committed to the view that the accounts were correct in every detail. Indeed I was impressed in my early studies of the resurrection stories by the seemingly intractable nature of the discrepancies.

The most obvious point of difficulty concerns the events of the first Easter morning, where Luke mentions at least five women at the tomb, while Mark refers to three, Matthew to two, John to one and Paul to none at all. John puts the visit to the tomb while it was still dark and Mark when the sun had risen. Mark's and Luke's messengers are men (Mark one, Luke two), while Matthew's and John's are angels (Matthew one, John two). Mark, Luke and John locate them inside the tomb, while Matthew's angel starts outside the tomb and finishes inside. Matthew tells of an appearance of Christ to a number of women who held his feet unrebuked, while John tells of an appearance to one woman who is forbidden to touch him. As to appearances to the Eleven, Matthew only records one in Galilee, while Luke only records an appearance at Jerusalem.

It is by no means easy to see how these things can be fitted together while remaining strictly faithful to what the writers say. But an insatiable curiosity made me want to know who did what and why each writer put things so. Reading all I could and studying the Greek text carefully, I gradually found many of the pieces of the jigsaw coming together. It now seems to me that these resurrection stories exhibit in a remarkable way the well-known characteristics of accurate and independent reporting, for superficially they show great disharmony, but on close examination the details gradually fall into place.

Though the resurrection of Jesus has been the fundamental tenet of Christian faith from its beginning, this tenet (sad to say) has been abandoned in recent years by many would-be Christian leaders. This includes a number of distinguished Anglican scholars who have either denied the bodily resurrection (e.g. the late Professor G.W.H. Lampe) or treated it as unimportant (e.g. Bishop J.A.T. Robinson) or declared its written records to be hopelessly contradictory (e.g. Professor C.F. Evans).[2] This justifies the inclusion of the present study in the Latimer House series.

Conclusions like those of Lampe and Evans are the result of a long process of critical study whereby the authority of parts of the gospel text has been eroded bit by bit till nothing dependable is left. The end result is a downgrading of the canonical gospels which may ultimately put them in the category of Christian romances or merely on a level with the gnostic gospels. This means an abandonment of the belief that the gospel-writers were competent witnesses of the events they relate. But to depart from this belief is to depart from historic Christianity into something quite other. If, however, it can be shown at the point where the evangelists are thought to be most at sixes and sevens that their accounts can be reconciled in detail and without strain, it suggests that much of the modern critical structure is on the wrong lines, and indeed that the God who revealed himself in Jesus Christ saw to it that the church had a trustworthy record of that tremendous happening.

Note
A short discussion of gospel criticism will be found in Appendix I. I have tried to keep matters requiring technical knowledge out of the body of the book and to confine them to the Notes at the back.

CHAPTER ONE

Setting the Scene: Jerusalem and Bethany

Our first need is an accurate knowledge of the lay-out of the stage on which the great drama was enacted. There are many details of first-century Jerusalem about which we are ignorant, but the general picture is clear, as a sketch map will show:

THE CITY: ITS WALLS, GATES AND RESIDENCES

The city was roughly one kilometre (a little over half a mile) square with strong walls, punctuated at intervals by gates. In general the city sloped from higher ground in the west down to the Kidron valley in the east. In the first century this was a less regular slope than is to be found today, because a second valley (the Tyropoean) lay between the upper city and the temple area. This Valley of the Cheesemakers, which was crossed by bridges, has since been filled with rubble to a depth of more than a hundred feet.

The tomb, it is generally agreed, was on the north side of the city. If, as most experts think, it was at or near the site of the present Church of the Holy Sepulchre, the wall must have been sharply indented at this point. This is not surprising in view of the unevenness of the terrain which had to be defended and the piecemeal enlargement of the city throughout the course of its history. The west section of the indented wall was probably part

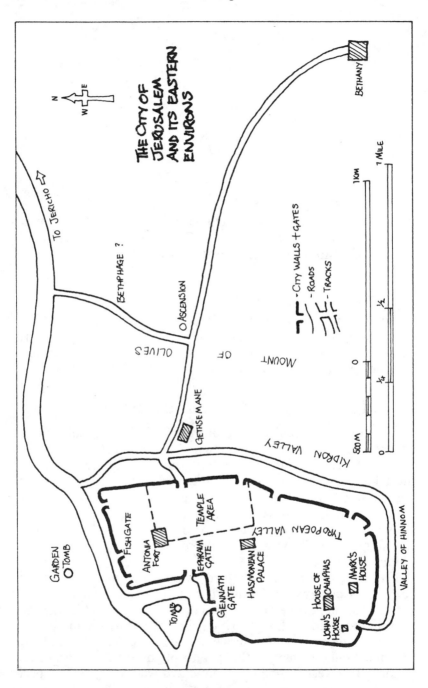

The City of Jerusalem and its Eastern Environs

of the ancient first wall which Josephus describes,[1] and the section running north was part of the more recently constructed second wall, built to give protection to the northern suburb. At least two gates gave access to the area where Joseph of Arimathea's garden lay, the more westerly one being known as the *Gennath Gate* (that is, the Gate of the Garden) and the more easterly one the *Ephraim Gate*. The *Fish Gate*, which is mentioned a number of times in the Old Testament[2](or something equivalent to it) was to be found apparently where the north wall crossed the Tyropoean valley.

The Hasmonean Palace, where Herod and his court stayed when in Jerusalem, was separated from the temple area by the Tyropoean valley. Access to the temple from the palace was by means of one of the bridges. Here Herod's steward Chuza and his wife Joanna would presumably have been staying.

The House of Caiaphas, where Peter's denial took place, was in the south-west part of the upper city, in a well-to-do area. It was not far from the traditional site of *John Mark's house*, the large upper room of which was the scene of the Last Supper, and which appears to have become the regular meeting place of the Christian church.[3]

John's house is more difficult to place. One tradition says that Mary lived out her days in John's house and 'fell asleep' in Jerusalem. The beautiful Church of the Dormition, which is in the same area as the house of Caiaphas and the house of Mark, commemorates the event. This sort of social proximity would have increased the likelihood of John being known to the high priest and also to such as Joseph of Arimathea and Nicodemus. But, although (as we shall see) the Zebedee family had a good little fish business in the city and were by no means poor, it is perhaps rather difficult to think that he lived in quite this sort of area. On the other hand there is one consideration which suggests that their house was not a very small one. It will be remembered that the place of meeting for the Last Supper was not known to the disciples beforehand; it was *secretly* arranged to take place in the upper room at John Mark's house.[4] This means that there was at least one other possible and more likely rendezvous known to them. We shall try to show in due course that the family of Jesus and the family of Zebedee were related[5] and that the natural expectation would have been that Jesus would keep the passover with the Zebedee family. As, however, there were probably nine people in the house already[6] and the addition of Jesus and his party would have meant a further thirteen, it would have entailed at least twenty-two people sitting down to the meal. That presupposes a house with a sizable room, even if not on the scale of Mark's large room which accommodated 120 people.[7]

Another possibility is that he lived somewhere near the fish market. The Fish Gate gave access to the so-called Suburb, which had only recently been enclosed within the city walls. The fish market may well have been in the older part of the city, but in this same general area. There exists at the present time a coffee shop to the south of the site of the Fish Gate which some tenaciously claim to be on the site of John's house.[8] But others think the tradition worthless. (It is not marked on the sketch map, but it would be just to the north of the Hasmonean palace.) The fact is, we really do not know whether there is any substance in either of the traditions.

I am inclined to favour the Dormition site and have chosen it for the map, because its location there would help to explain two important matters: (a) Its proximity would render more intelligible John's ready access to the house of Caiaphas. (b) Since the other site is near the Hasmonean palace, it would be somewhat less easy from that position to account for the fact that the women leaving the tomb did not meet John and Peter on their way there. The Dormition site explains it at once. Furthermore, it needs to be remembered that the city then, as now, must have been criss-crossed with many narrow streets, so that there were usually several possible ways of getting from one place to another.

OUTSIDE THE CITY

To visualise the topographical features it is probably best to imagine oneself at a high point in the upper (or western) part of the city, and from there looking eastward. Along the skyline can be seen the ridge of the *Mount of Olives*. The Mount of Olives is about as far removed from the ordinary person's idea of a mountain as could be. It has no peak, being more like an undulating plateau with three gently rounded summits. It hides from view the great rift valley through which the river Jordan runs and the mountains of Moab and Ammon which lie beyond.

Having gained an idea of the contours of the summit of Olivet one can then walk down from the upper city and enter the temple area. Crossing over to its far side one can take a closer look at the terrain to the east of the city from a vantage point on the boundary wall. To the left can be seen the line of the Roman road which skirts the northern wall of the city, dips down into the Kidron valley and then ascends the steep rise over the Mount of Olives. It passes north of the village of *Bethphage*[9] on the plateau summit and then begins the deep descent into the rift valley till it reaches Jericho. The Brook Kidron is an intermittent winter wadi.

Looking now ahead, a rough track can be seen which again ascends out of the Kidron valley and up the hillside and then leads gently down to *Bethany*, a distance in all of nearly two miles. Just across the Kidron valley near the point where the track begins its ascent is the *Garden of Gethsemane*. Gethsemane means 'oil press' and it is more of an orchard than an ornamental garden. Surrounded by high walls it not only has privacy and the welcome shade of its olive trees, but its olives make it a place of profit to its owner.

If one now clambers up the track, one finds that at the top it divides. To the left a path leads to Bethphage and the Jericho road, and the other path goes on down to Bethany. In this delightful situation at the top of the rise the Galileans used to set up their camps at festival time. It would seem that Jesus' party encamped or lodged in or near Bethany on his last visit to Jerusalem. They came up from Jericho by the main road and ascended the Mount of Olives from the east side, till they reached the track which led them through Bethphage and on towards Bethany. For his entry into the city, Jesus would have walked back till near Bethphage, ridden through the village on the donkey and down the main road into Jerusalem.

Looking back now from the summit of Olivet at the point where the paths divide there is a glorious view of the city spread out below like a picture. Coming out of the city gates can be seen paths which make it possible to walk round the city outside the walls. After the Last Supper the disciples may have left the city by one of the southern gates or they may have walked through the city and left by a gate on the east.

Galilee, which also figures in our story, is of course a territory fifty or more miles north of Jerusalem, a two to three day journey for those on foot.

THE TOMB

Its Location: The Holy Sepulchre?

The site of Jesus' tomb must be presumed to be within the Church of the Holy Sepulchre unless decisive evidence to the contrary is forthcoming. According to the contemporary historian Eusebius (in his *Life of Constantine* III.25–29) the emperor was led to believe that the tomb of Jesus would be found beneath a heathen temple which had been built in Jerusalem in about AD 135. No one for nearly two centuries had seen what lay beneath its pavements and underlying soil, but when in AD 325 Constantine's workmen dug down they found a cave tomb, which must at one time have been situated outside the city, since no burials were allowed within the walls. That a burial place should have been looked for *and found* beneath a heathen temple *within the city* is strong evidence that the Christian community had retained a firm tradition as to where Jesus was buried.

The Garden Tomb?

The present north wall of the city brings the Church of the Holy Sepulchre within its boundaries. Further north outside the wall is a large rock-hewn tomb set in a delightful garden which is deservedly loved by many tourists as giving a beautiful idea of what the burial place of Jesus might have looked like. But seriously to claim that this Garden Tomb was Christ's burial place would require four conditions, three of which would be very difficult to establish.

First, there would need to be decisive archaeological evidence that the traditional site was wrong, for instance by showing that it lies inside the north wall of Herodian Jerusalem. The excavations of Kathleen Kenyon in the 1960s seem to have shown decisively that it did in fact lie outside.[10]

Second, it would need to be shown that in the case of the Garden Tomb the archaeological evidence fitted convincingly the biblical claim that the tomb was newly hewn in Joseph of Arimathea's time. At present archaeologists differ enormously in their views. C. Kopp in his standard work, *The Holy Places of the Gospels*,[11] regards it as dating long after New Testament times: "The grave is part of a cemetery of St. Etienne belonging to the Byzantine period." J. Wilkinson, *Jerusalem as Jesus Knew It*,[12] dates the tombs in that area very roughly around the time of Christ: "Their style shows only that they could have been made some time between about 200 BC and AD 200." An Israeli archaeologist has recently come to the conclusion that it is to be dated long before New Testament times: "This is in all likelihood a Jewish family tomb dating to the days of the Second Temple or possibly the days of the First."[13]

Third, one would need to establish that the Garden Tomb fitted the biblical data. This is the least difficult thing to establish — it does fit well.

Fourth, one would need to establish that of the hundreds of rock tombs around Jerusalem there were not others which fitted the data equally well. After all, it is on the face of it long odds that a tomb discovered in the nineteenth century, concerning which there was no tradition connecting it with Jesus, should in fact be his. It would be necessary to show that there were no rivals with equally good claims. A verdict on this matter would require specialist expertise. It needs to be remembered that the great interest in the Garden Tomb was stimulated by its link with the so-called Gordon's Calvary. General Gordon was a popular hero and a devout amateur Bible student, who supported his identification with a somewhat fanciful piece of typology. He argued that, because in the ritual of the tabernacle sacrificial victims were killed to the north-west of the altar, therefore in the antitype the actual sacrifice of Christ would have taken place to the north-west of the altar in Herod's temple, which was situated where the Mosque of El Omar now stands.[14] It so happens that a line drawn north-west from the mosque strikes a limestone cliff face adjacent to the Garden Tomb, which has a somewhat skull-like appearance. Whether this soft, easily weathered rock has preserved a skull-like appearance for 2,000 years, no one knows. But to some it seemed to account for the description of the site of the crucifixion as the Place of a Skull, which all the evangelists use. All this provides a precarious foundation on which to build an identification.

The Construction of Jesus' Tomb

The Holy Sepulchre has for many centuries been encased in a massive marble structure, known as the Rotunda, which makes it impossible to see what the original tomb was like. Indeed much of the surrounding rock was cut away when Constantine built the first church there in the fourth century, and more was deliberately destroyed by non-Christians in the eleventh century.[15] J.P. Kane thinks that the approximate location of Jesus' tomb may well have been remembered till the time of Constantine, but he does not think that the Holy Sepulchre can be the actual tomb.[16] His argument is built on the earliest description of the Holy Sepulchre which we possess, which was given by Bishop Arculf who visited Jerusalem at the beginning of the eighth century.[17] Kane considers Arculf's tomb to have had a trough-like recess of a type hardly found in Herodian times.

The characteristic Herodian tomb has a low entry, closed by a large, roughly shaped stone, which is pushed (like a bottle-stopper) right into the hole. (The millstone type, flush with the wall, running in a sloping channel and covering up the entrance, is very rare.) Often a central pit provides standing room, and usually there are flat ledges round the walls where bodies may be temporarily laid and oven-like recesses in the walls into which they will finally be put. A number have antechambers and these too usually have one or more flat rock-hewn ledges. While these are the commonest characteristics of Herodian tombs, it needs to be stressed that there are wide differences of design at any one period (varying particularly with the wealth of the owner) and often there are great uncertainties about dating.

To fulfil the conditions described in the gospels, the tomb must have been roomy and it must have been entered by a low opening. On entering, the grave space was apparently on the right and was partially visible from the entrance. This grave-space could either have been at floor level, or it could have been on a so-called 'bench', a flat surface perhaps at waist level. In either case the angels could have sat one where the head and one where the feet of Jesus had lain. The accompanying diagram gives an idea of the simplest design compatible with the data.

The Garden Tomb is a little more complicated than this, but it too gives a vivid idea of what the original tomb might have

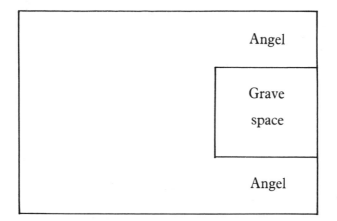

Entrance

looked like. To those who can go to the Holy Land an unhurried visit is heartily recommended as a means of bringing the whole story to life.

CHAPTER TWO

The Actors: Mary Magdalene

Having seen the layout of the Jerusalem area we must now look at the individual actors and see what is known about them. There are twenty-three actors to be considered: the five women visitors to the tomb, eleven apostles, Cleopas, the Lord's Mother and her four sons, and John Mark, the evangelist. Pride of place must be given to Mary Magdalene, who is named first by all the evangelists and who was the first human being to see the risen Jesus. If, in giving her a chapter of her own, disproportionate space seems to be allotted to her, this is not because the identification here adopted is essential to the argument. It did have an important place in building up the suggested reconstruction of the events, but, as will be seen, this particular identification proves in the end to be dispensable. Nonetheless, it is a matter of great intrinsic interest to all who love the human element in the gospel story to try to trace her story.

With the exception of the Mother of our Lord, Mary Magdalene is the most favoured woman in the Bible. Yet apart from a brief mention by Luke of her healing and of her service to Jesus in Galilee,[1] she appears in the story as suddenly as a meteor, shines brightly for a moment, and then disappears for ever. If this is all we know of her, we can form very little idea of her character or of her story.

There is, however, an ancient and tenaciously-held tradition that Mary Magdalene was the 'sinner' whose repentance is so movingly portrayed in Luke 7:36–50. This young woman had evidently listened to the teaching of Jesus and had decided to forsake her present life in order to follow him. Jesus was known to be dining with a Pharisee named Simon and she determined publicly to declare her new allegiance. Braving the stares and sneers of the onlookers, she stole into the room with a flask of ointment in her hands and came up behind him as he reclined on the divan. Suddenly and uncontrollably tears of penitence and joy began to stream down her face and fell upon his feet. Forgetting all proprieties she hastily let down her long hair and began to try to wipe the tears away. She then started kissing his feet and finally she poured the ointment over them – the ointment which had been intended for his head. In the subsequent exchange Jesus gave her the unique commendation: 'she loved much'.

If this woman is identified with Mary Magdalene, the possibility of a second identification is at once raised. For if Mary Magdalene is the woman whom Luke describes as anointing Jesus, the question inevitably arises as to her relation with the woman described by Matthew, Mark and John as anointing him.[2] John makes it clear that she too was a Mary, the sister of Martha and Lazarus, who lived in Bethany.[3] The name Mary (or more strictly Miriam – after the sister of Moses) was easily the commonest girl's name at the time (there seem to have been at least seven different Marys mentioned in the New Testament), so it would have been no great coincidence if there had been two women of this name performing a similar action. But are there in fact grounds for believing Luke's sinner to be the same person as Mary of Bethany, and for believing Mary of Bethany to be the same person as Mary Magdalene?

Tradition gives no clear guidance. There is indeed a long tradition that equates them, immensely strong in the West (though not in the East) at least from the sixth to the nineteenth century.[4] It may have reached right back to apostolic times without a break, though this can be neither proved nor disproved. Nor has this tradition died out in modern times, in spite of a sharp reaction against it in the nineteenth century. This reaction was due particularly to the influence of Descartes' philosophy upon biblical and historical criticism. Descartes in seeking a solid philosophical foundation, determined to doubt everything he could doubt and build on what remained. Many New Testament scholars have adopted this principle of maximum doubt and so have ruthlessly rejected a number of widely accepted notions (which are not in themselves improbable) as undemonstrable and worthless.[5] This fate has fallen to the Mary Magdalene tradition, but not all scholars have been persuaded that its dismissal is right. A. O'Rahilly, writing in 1949, mentioned twenty 'recent' commentators who identified the three women: Bernard, Bird, Cladder, Corluy, Delatte, Didon, Fonck, Fouard, Hetzenauer, Kastner, Kaulen, Lattey, Le Camus, Lemonnyer, Lesêtre, Maas, Ollivier, Pope, Sepp, Trench.[6] All these writers (including O'Rahilly himself) after carefully studying the data, evidently felt that the identifications, though incapable of proof, were none the less right. We can only set out the pros and cons and see what impression they make.

It must be remembered that the presupposition of this study is that the evangelists were honest and well informed men, writing gospels which God purposed should be used for the instruction of his church. It is therefore right to accept the records as they stand as reliable, unless there is compelling reason to the contrary. There are of course many scholars who believe that these and other traditions about Jesus have been seriously distorted in transmission and that one story has been cross-fertilised by another, so that we cannot put any trust in the details of the various accounts. Our presupposition, however, demands that we should dismiss no detail until we have fully explored the possibility of taking the narratives just as they stand. It will be convenient to consider in turn the relation of Mary of Bethany to Luke's sinner and then of her relation to Mary Magdalene.

WAS LUKE'S SINNER MARY OF BETHANY?

In order to understand the relation between the anointing in Galilee by the sinner and the anointing in Bethany by Mary, we must first grasp the significance of the wiping of Jesus' feet with the woman's hair. *For a woman to let her hair down in the presence of men was considered utterly disgraceful* and some rabbis considered it a just ground for divorce.[7] Yet this is what Luke reports of the sinner in Galilee and what John reports of Mary of Bethany. In the Galilee incident her action was not so remarkable, because (though inwardly a reformed person) she was still disreputable in the eyes of those who saw her, and in any case her act was an unpremeditated response to an unexpected accident. But in the second instance, the action was planned and deliberate. The woman was not drying away tears, she first poured ointment on his feet and then inexplicably wiped it off. This was evidently of particular significance to John, because he mentions it in two different contexts – once in chapter 12 when narrating the incident itself, but also in the previous chapter (11:2) where he is introducing Mary for the first time: 'It was Mary who anointed the Lord with ointment *and wiped his feet with her hair.*'

Incidentally, there is often thought to be a discrepancy between John's account of the anointing in Bethany and that of Matthew and Mark, for the latter say that Mary anointed his head, whereas John says that she anointed his feet. There is no reason why both should not be true, and interestingly John seems to betray an awareness that this may have been so. For in his initial introduction of Mary in chapter 11 he does not say, 'It was Mary who anointed his *feet* with ointment and wiped them with her hair,' but, 'It was Mary who anointed *the Lord* with ointment and wiped his feet with her hair.' This could quite well mean the anointing of both head and feet. For if the sentence had ended with a full-stop after 'anointed the Lord with ointment', the reader would have taken it for granted that she had anointed his head – the head being the normal and natural part of the body to anoint. (It will be recalled how Jesus had said that those who fast should disguise the fact by anointing their heads, and how he had rebuked Simon with the words 'You gave me no water for my feet ... You did not anoint my head.')[8] Having mentioned the anointing of the Lord, John then goes on to call attention to its peculiar feature: Mary 'anointed the Lord <u>and</u> wiped his feet with her hair.' This is a point he wished to emphasise.

With this background in mind, it is possible to set out four propositions which together seem to point to the identity of Mary and the sinner.

1.   *There were two anointings.* The incident related by Luke and the incident related by Matthew, Mark and John were certainly

not the same event. Luke's anointing was in Galilee during the Galilean ministry, the other was in Bethany just before the passion. Luke's woman was a sinner, the other (according to John) was the devout sister of Lazarus. Luke's central motif is the woman's penitence and tears, the other sees the act as a preparation for Jesus' burial.

2. *The same woman did both anointings.* The sense of John's words is: 'It was Mary (the one who anointed the Lord with ointment and wiped his feet with her hair) whose brother Lazarus was ill.' This implies that there was only one woman known to the church who fitted that description, which seems to require that it was the same woman who did similar acts on the two occasions. It is interesting that John introduces her in this way *before* he relates the story. This could mean that he expects many of his readers to know the story even before he tells it. But it would be like John if he had a double reference in mind – a reference back to the story of the sinner woman of Galilee (which he expected many of his readers to know, whether from Luke 7 or from oral teaching); and a reference forward to a second deed by the same woman (which he is shortly to recount). If (as may be argued) John is deliberately supplementing the synoptists, it may even be his way of linking Luke's story with that of Matthew and Mark.

3. *The second anointing can be explained as a re-enactment and completion of the first.* The first anointing, as we saw, did not go according to plan. She had intended to anoint Jesus in the ordinary way on his head, when suddenly she had burst into tears which had streamed down onto his bare feet as he reclined on the divan. Without thinking she committed the scandalous indecency of letting her hair down in order to dry his feet. In her confusion she then poured the ointment over them. But how can we explain the second action, when she deliberately repeated the disgraceful misdemeanour and let down her hair again, and this time anointed both head and feet? The anointing of his head looks like the completion of the earlier act which went awry; and the anointing of his feet and the wiping *off* of the ointment looks like a sort of re-enactment of the previous scene, presumably an act of profound thankfulness and love at the recollection of that wonderful day when Jesus brought her back into the fold.

4. *So to relate the two anointings enables us to trace the outline of a coherent story of Mary's past.* It means that Mary's actual home

was not in Galilee, but in Bethany, the Judean village a couple of miles east of Jerusalem. It would seem to have been a home where Jesus received a particularly warm welcome. John remarks quite simply that 'Jesus loved Martha and her sister and Lazarus.'[9] It may well have been a haven where he stayed, not only on this last visit to Jerusalem, but also on his earlier visits. Yet Mary had left home and had somehow become a notorious 'sinner' in one of the towns of Galilee. (We should probably not think of her as a street prostitute, but as a person of poise and charm whose favours were sought by the upper ranks of society.)

It is easy to let the imagination run riot in attempting to reconstruct the story, but it cannot be far from the truth, if we see her as a great contrast to her older sister Martha: Martha practical and fulfilled in managing one of the more distinguished homes in the village; Mary attractive, adventurous and visionary, yet frustrated in her role as second fiddle, moody, longing to get out to see the world and enjoy life. It is easy to see how her leaving of home, at first so exciting and enjoyable, all turned sour on her. It is not surprising that when she turned back her conversion went very deep indeed.

After she had been reunited with her family, both Luke and John give glimpses of her spiritual intuition and of her devotion to Jesus. She was the one who earned her sister's rebuke and Jesus' commendation, when she sat at the Lord's feet and listened to his teaching, while Martha toiled at the domestic chores.[10] She was the one who gloomily stayed indoors when Martha went out to meet Jesus after the death of Lazarus. The mourners from Jerusalem stayed with her, but on hearing that Jesus had summoned her, she went out quickly and they followed her. On coming to him she fell at his feet weeping. It was on seeing Mary and the other mourners in this state that 'Jesus wept', being deeply moved in spirit and troubled.[11] In the closing days of the Lord's life, Mary seems to have had a unique rapport with him. When she anoints him he declares that 'she has done a beautiful thing to me', she has kept the ointment 'for the day of my burial', 'wherever this gospel is preached in the whole world, what this woman has done will be told in memory of her.'[12] Within Mary were deeps of intuition and devotion shared by no one else.

Such is the case for the first identification, which, if the details of the narratives are taken with full seriousness, seems difficult to gainsay. The case against amounts to one obstinate fact: *Luke does not even hint at such an identification*. As this is also the principal argument against the second identification, it will be discussed later.

WAS MARY MAGDALENE MARY OF BETHANY?

There are again four propositions which seem to favour this identification.

1. *Magdala provides a suitable location for Luke's sinner.* Magdalene means 'of Magdala', Magdala being a town on the western shore of the Sea of Galilee. It was, and is, a delectable spot, doubtless very attractive to Roman officers and officials on leave. It was famed for its wealth and its moral corruption.[13] If Mary of Bethany did in fact take to prostitution in one of the Galilean towns, none is more likely than Magdala. If Magdala was her place of residence when she became a follower of Jesus, it would have been very natural to have distinguished her from the myriad other Miriams by dubbing her Magdalene.[14]

2. *Luke's introduction of Mary Magdalene at the beginning of chapter 8 would be explained if chapter 7 is the story of her conversion.* Luke's account of the transformation of the woman in chapter 7 is followed immediately by this paragraph:

> Soon afterward he went on through cities and villages, preaching and bringing the good news of the kingdom of God. And the twelve were with him, and also some women who had been healed of evil spirits and infirmities: Mary, called Magdalene, from whom seven demons had gone out, and Joanna, the wife of Chuza, Herod's steward, and Susanna, and many others, who provided for them out of their means.

Why is that statement inserted at this point, where it introduces, not a period of journeyings, but a somewhat static period during which Jesus is based on Capernaum? It would be explained if this paragraph were connected in Luke's mind with the incident which precedes it. If he had known that the transformed woman had almost at once joined the other women in costly service of Jesus, this would explain how Mary came to get her name, why she is given pride of place here as the first-named of the women, and why Luke mentions the ministrations of the women at this point in his narrative. The considerable difficulties faced by those who wish to explain it otherwise are discussed at length in Appendix II (p. 129)

3. *Mary Magdalene and Mary of Bethany never appear on the stage together.* We have successively:

the sinner's conversion (Luke 7)
Mary Magdalene with the itinerating women (Luke 8)
Martha and Mary welcoming Jesus to their home (Luke 10)
Jesus raises their brother Lazarus (John 11)
Mary anoints Jesus at Bethany (Matt. 26, Mark 14, John 12)
Mary Magdalene stands at the cross
               witnesses the burial
               visits the tomb
               sees the Lord.

4. *These scenes dovetail into one another, producing a coherent story and portraying a consistent character.* As we shall see,[15] Jesus and his disciples spent the nights of the first part of Holy Week at Bethany in the closest touch with the family of Lazarus. They must have all shared the ever-sharpening sense of doom. It is hard to believe that the Mary, who a week before had been told that her beautiful deed would be remembered throughout the world, played no part in the resurrection story, but that the privilege of first seeing the risen Lord was given to another, almost unknown, Mary. It is possible of course that there were two greatly privileged women, but the supposition seems unnecessary. The impulsive, emotional, devoted, discerning, privileged woman of the earlier stories, whom others were wont to follow, reappears in the vivid characterisation of the resurrection stories. She is mentioned first, she dashes off to Peter and John, she lingers in the house, she returns to the tomb and stands there weeping. She sees angels, she senses a presence, she hears Jesus utter her name. She cries 'Rabboni' and throwing herself at his feet clings to him. Why invent another Mary when Mary of Bethany is so perfectly portrayed? The one who loved much, the one whose action was to be remembered wherever the gospel was preached throughout the whole world, was also surely the one who first saw the Lord.

This coherence of story and consistency of character could well explain the persistence in the church of belief in the identity of the women, for close study brings to light nothing out of keeping with it.

Three arguments have been brought against this identification.
1. *Mary is shown as a resident of Bethany, not itinerating like Mary Magdalene.* But no one would suggest that all the women accompanied Jesus all the time. If he was planning to visit Bethany with his large party, Mary would naturally go ahead to help prepare for their coming. When it is remembered that she seems to have had a unique intuition about his death, and that she elicited the Lord's 'Wherever the gospel is preached in the whole world, what she has done will be told in memory of her,'[16] it is better to see Mary as one who had kept close company with him and had heard his repeated predictions of the passion, than as a village girl living a life of sheltered domesticity.

2. *To equate Mary Magdalene 'from whom seven demons had gone out' with Luke's 'sinner' is to confuse two quite different things: demon-possession and sin.* Could Luke have spoken of release from seven demons when he meant deliverance from her 'many' sins? There certainly seems to be no place for two great crises in the life of the unregenerate Mary, a literal exorcism in addition to her own deep repentance as described by Luke. But for a girl from a devout home, in a society which had high standards of sexual morality, to fall as low as she did would undoubtedly have been regarded as a triumph for demonic powers, and her deliverance could have been described (whether intended euphemistically or literally) as the coming out of demons. Indeed Luke himself quotes Jesus as saying that a man may be inhabited by an *unclean* spirit, which, after it has been driven out, takes seven spirits more *evil* than itself and returns to him.[17] Such 'spirits' are the authors of uncleanness and sin, and it was of such 'evil spirits' that Joanna and her friends were said to have been healed. A. O'Rahilly[18] justly remarks that the contrast between demoniacal possession and sin, which are said to be essentially different concepts, is greatly exaggerated. He refers to *The Testaments of the Twelve Patriarchs* (first century AD ?)[19] which says: 'Seven spirits are appointed against man and they are the leaders in the works of youth'. These are then enumerated as fornication, gluttony, fighting, chicanery, pride, lying, injustice. All this suggests that Luke's description of Mary Magdalene could well be used of the woman whose sins were 'many'.

3. *Luke could not have known the identity of his three characters without giving some hint of the fact.* Far and away the greatest

objection to these identifications is undoubtedly the fact that Luke speaks of the sinner in chapter 7, of Mary Magdalene in chapter 8, of Mary sister of Martha in chapter 10 and of Mary Magdalene again in chapter 24, without ever saying that they are the same person. This raises some general questions about the processes of gospel-writing and some particular questions about this immediate issue.

We must recognise that arguments from silence are notoriously untrustworthy. The fact that a writer gives no hint of something is no proof that he does not know it. No one knows how Luke put his special material together. It is likely that he taught and preached most of it many times. Some of it he may have received in writing, much of it he may have committed to writing at different periods of his missionary work. When he came to compose his gospel presumably he (like most authors) juggled his written material around – discarding, revising, adding, sewing together. His joins would not always be perfect and his connections of thought would not always be obvious. This consideration alone should make us very chary about saying that Luke would almost certainly have identified his characters.

Another point to notice is that in a number of cases the identity of the woman is irrelevant to the message of the story. It is of intense interest to us to know who she may have been, but it would not have increased the impact of the story if the evangelists had substituted a name in place of their simple references to 'a woman'.[20]

Now to deal with particular questions:

(a) *If the sinner was Mary Magdalene, why does not Luke say so?* May it not have been the same sense of delicacy which kept Luke from using the actual term 'prostitute'[21] (though this is almost certainly what he meant, even if she was not a common street prostitute), which also kept him from saying explicitly that the respected Magdalene had once followed that trade? The New Testament generally is very restrained about former sins of converts. Maybe Luke wished to magnify the grace of God in Mary's marvellous turn-about, but did not wish publicly to advertise the sordid past of a saintly woman.

(b) *Why does Luke drop the designation Magdalene in chapter 10?* If it is true that Mary got her name from her former place of residence rather than from her real home, it might well have been a little confusing, not to say irrelevant, to have spoken of her in the same breath as 'of Bethany' and 'of Magdala'. Therefore in the context of her home it is not surprising that Luke (like John) calls her simply Mary. It would incidentally have upset the balance of the superb little anecdote if Luke had at this point called attention to Mary's lurid past.

(c) *Why do Luke and John in the closing chapters (in common with Matthew and Mark) consistently add the term Magdalene?* The short answer is probably that she was almost always called this as the most convenient way of distinguishing her from all the other Marys. (It has to be remembered that three of the four women at the cross were Marys.) It is only in Bethany contexts that the term is *not* used.

But there may have been a more subtle factor at work. The question has long been discussed why no mention is made anywhere in the synoptic gospels of the raising of Lazarus in Bethany, in spite of the crucial role it plays in John's story. A plausible answer is that Jerusalem was hostile towards followers of Jesus and it would have been an unnecessary and possibly dangerous embarrassment to the family to have mentioned Lazarus while he was still alive.[22] The use therefore by the synoptists of the designation Mary of Magdala in the Jerusalem context conveniently directs attention away from the family's home on the outskirts of the city.

So it seems that the case for the threefold identification is substantial and the case against it relatively insubstantial. There is every justification for using it as a working hypothesis. It has been necessary to establish the identity of Mary Magdalene at such length because the world of scholarship is so heavily inclined to the view that it is a convenient ploy for novelists and playwrights, but historically worthless. This has been the case, not only with radical critics, but even with staunch conservatives like Alfred Edersheim and William Hendriksen. We submit, however, that if the accounts are reliable this identification is difficult to avoid.

The significance for our story of the identification of the three women is that it locates Mary Magdalene's home in Bethany. It should be noticed, however, that the identification is in no way essential to the harmonization of the narratives – the harmony would be just as complete (though more conjectural) if, say, Mary Magdalene was a friend of the Bethany family and stayed with them for the festival.

CHAPTER THREE

The Other Actors

To the casual reader Matthew's 'other Mary', Mark's 'Salome' and John's 'Clopas' seem obscure and rather unimportant figures. To the careful student, however, they prove exceptionally interesting. A key to their identification is to be found in the descriptions of the women at the crucifixion given by Matthew, Mark and John.[1] Matthew and Mark (whose accounts at this point run parallel) identify three women watching at a distance, while John mentions Jesus' mother and three other women standing by the cross. It is natural to suppose that the same three women are referred to in each case and that they came forward with the Lord's mother to support her in the final farewell. If the women are the same in each case, we get the following descriptions:

1. Mary Magdalene — so called in all three gospels.
2. One called
by Matthew:	'the mother of the sons of Zebedee'.
by Mark:	'Salome'.
by John:	'Jesus' mother's sister'.[2]
3. Mary, called
by Matthew:	'the mother of James and Joseph' (or in many manuscripts 'Joses', which is another form of the same patriarch's name) or 'the other Mary'.

by Mark:	'the mother of James the younger and of Joses' or 'the mother of Joses' or 'the mother of James'.
by John:	'the wife of Clopas'.

This enables us to draw up genealogical trees for Salome and the other Mary.

SALOME AND HER FAMILY

Salome's relationships may be seen thus:

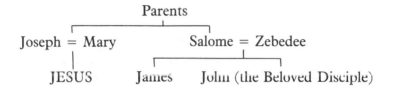

This means that Salome is, on the one hand, the sister of the Lord's mother — that is to say, Jesus' aunt; and, on the other hand, mother of the two leading disciples, James and John. This makes John first cousin to Jesus.

These two sisters and their families were evidently very close indeed. The Zebedee family had a fishing business in or near Capernaum, and shortly before the beginning of his Galilean ministry it would seem that Jesus and his family moved to the same town, presumably to be near them.[3] This suggests that Jesus knew his aunt Salome well, and also his cousins James and John. John in his gospel (according to the traditional and most satisfactory interpretation) gives himself the extraordinary description of '*the* disciple whom Jesus loved'. The simplest explanation of this otherwise arrogant title is that these two cousins had in fact been lifelong friends.[4] If Salome was a year or two older than Mary and they both married at the usual age, Salome's second-born might well have been the same age as Mary's firstborn. It is not perhaps surprising then that Salome and her sons cherished hopes that the two of them might have privileged places, one at his right hand and one at his left, in his kingdom.[5]

The mother of Jesus plays no direct part in the actual resurrection narratives,[6] though her presence in the home of the

beloved disciple[7] probably had an influence on the course of
events. Of the brothers of Jesus at this time we know practically
nothing. As practising Jews they were presumably in Jerusalem
for the festival. We know that they did not eat the passover with
Jesus, being (we must presume) still in a state of unbelief about
him. One would expect to find them staying at the home of their
Zebedee relatives for the festival, but they might have decided to
make themselves scarce, when they became aware of their
brother's acute danger. The question of the relationship between
Jesus and his four brothers, James, Joses (or Joseph), Simon and
Judas is discussed in Appendix III (pp. 132), where the earlier
history of the family is sketched out.

THE OTHER MARY AND HER FAMILY

The other Mary's relationships may be seen diagrammatically
thus:

The other Mary = Clopas (Jn)

James (Mt, Lk; 'James the younger', Mk)

Joseph or Joses (Mt, Mk)

This is straightforward enough: the other Mary was married to
Clopas and had two sons, James the Younger and Joses. But
when it comes to the further exploration of the other Mary's
family, things become complex.

James the Younger

Nothing more is known about Joses, but there are two pieces
of information about James which merit investigation. His
designation is literally 'James the little', which some have taken
to refer to his stature or physique, but it seems unlikely that this

somewhat undignified description would have stuck as the standard designation of a church leader.[8] It was quite common in the contemporary Greek for a positive adjective like 'little' to be used for the comparative 'less', so the Revised Standard Version would seem to be right to take it in this sense of 'less in age' and to translate it as 'James the younger'. But 'younger' than whom? The lists of the apostles[9] provide an obvious answer, for there were two apostles called James. One of these, a son of Zebedee, belonged to the innermost apostolic circle, so it would be natural to suppose that he was 'James the elder', and that the other lesser known apostle was 'James the younger', son of Clopas and Mary.

Clopas/Alphaeus/Cleopas

This second James is described in all the four lists of the apostles as 'of Alphaeus', which would normally mean 'son of Alphaeus'. This raises the question whether Clopas and Alphaeus are two versions of the same name. They could well be two versions of the Aramaic name usually transliterated Chalphai.[10] The first letter of the name is a guttural which could be transliterated in Greek either as a *k*, giving Clopas, or as an *h*. *h* is represented in Greek by a small sign known as a rough breathing, which was often dropped both in speaking and in writing, so giving the Greek Halphaios or Alphaios, which was Latinized as Alphaeus. There is thus no great difficulty in equating James the son of Clopas with James the son of Alphaeus, that is, with James the younger. This means that the tentative identification of James the younger as an apostle and the tentative identification of Clopas with Alphaeus reinforce one another. Together the two seeming probabilities add up to one firm probability.

Further, Clopas can be equated with Cleopas.[11] Cleopas (a shortened form of Cleopatros) is the nearest genuine Greek name to Clopas, and it seems likely that Luke is referring to this same person when narrating the Emmaus story. He could have adopted this form in preference to the form derived from the Aramaic in writing up his story for his Greek-speaking readers. But if Cleopas is Clopas, a flood of light is thrown on these two otherwise obscure figures. It would mean that the first man to see the risen Lord was husband of the woman who stood by the cross, who watched at the burial, who came early to the tomb and who herself had seen the risen Lord. Further, these two would be parents of one of the apostles, and would have been at the heart of the company who followed Jesus. This equation of Cleopas with Clopas gives him a position in the circle of Jesus which makes it less surprising that he should have seen the risen Christ before any of the apostles.

Further knowledge of Clopas and his family can be gained from church history. The great historian of the early church, Eusebius of Caesarea, who wrote his *Ecclesiastical History* towards the beginning of the fourth century, says:

> After the martyrdom of James, and the capture of Jerusalem, which immediately followed, it is reported, that those of the apostles and the disciples of our Lord, that were yet surviving, came together from all parts with those that were related to our Lord according to the flesh .... They all unanimously declared Simeon the son of Clopas, *of whom mention is made in the sacred volume*, as worthy of the episcopal seat there. They say he was the cousin of our Saviour, for Hegesippus asserts that *Clopas was the brother of Joseph*.[12]

This Hegesippus, whom Eusebius quotes verbatim a number of times, was a second-century historian. He was a widely travelled man, a converted Jew, probably a native of Palestine; there seems no reason to doubt that he was a good authority. Eusebius identifies this Clopas as the character mentioned in Scripture, and adds the interesting information that he was brother of Joseph, the Virgin Mary's husband, so making Simeon 'the cousin of our Saviour'. This would mean, firstly, that Clopas/ Cleopas/Alphaeus was uncle to Jesus; secondly, that Simeon was brother to James the younger and Joses; and, thirdly, that Simeon, James and Joses were first cousins to Jesus. The relationships can be seen in the genealogical table on p. 40, which also includes the brothers of Jesus.[13]

For the purpose of piecing the story together it is useful to notice these connections between the family of Joseph and Mary, the family of Clopas and Mary and the family of Zebedee and Salome. Pilgrims to overcrowded Jerusalem would almost as a matter of course lodge with relatives where possible. This means that we should expect to find them all in John's house over the festival. It is also valuable to recognize Mary and Clopas as parents of the apostle James the younger, for this establishes their interest in the disciples who had fled on the night of Jesus' arrest. It will be noticed that Salome and Mary of Clopas are both of the generation prior to that of the thirty-year old Jesus, whereas the attractive Magdalene must have been much younger. It is reasonable to suppose that they were stabler and less impulsive than she.

JOANNA

Joanna is mentioned only by Luke, first as one of the well-to-do women who provided for Jesus and his party 'out of their means' during his Galilean ministry and then as one of those who visited the tomb.[14] Her husband was 'steward' to Herod Antipas, ruler of Galilee and Peraea. His status would probably have been roughly that of finance minister or possibly that of manager of the royal estates.[15] He would have been a permanent and senior member of Herod's court and so he and his wife would normally have lived at the royal residence — when in Galilee in Tiberias and on their occasional visits to Jerusalem at the Hasmonean palace.[16] Belonging to the upper crust of Jewish society Joanna was probably well known to Joseph of Arimathea and to Nicodemus.

THE BELOVED DISCIPLE

There is no need to spend time on the various implausible modern suggestions which identify the beloved disciple and 'the other disciple' with Lazarus or Mark or the rich young ruler, or which spirit him away as a non-historical ideal figure who symbolises the true follower of Christ. The traditional identification with the apostle John has no effective rival. There is no need either to outline his place in the gospel story as a whole, which is well known. We shall concentrate our attention on his role in Jerusalem in the closing days of the ministry.

Two important and related facts stand out: John 'was known to the high priest' — known sufficiently well to him and to the maidservant at the door to be able to enter his premises unchallenged — and he had a home in Jerusalem to which he immediately took Jesus' mother at the time of the crucifixion.[17]

GENEALOGICAL TABLE

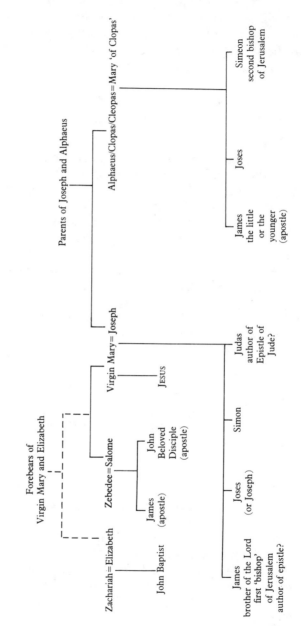

This means that the Galilean fisherman had had two foci of operation. His roots were in Capernaum, but, as his intimate knowledge of Jerusalem and its happenings shows, he also spent much of his time in the capital.

There are two possible reasons for this. One is that John may have been a priest, a *kohen*. To be a priest was simply a matter of heredity, of being a descendant in the male line from Aaron. As in Judaism today, there were many Cohens fulfilling all sorts of secular avocations. But all priests would be entitled to do a spell of duty in the temple twice or perhaps three times a year. The evidence that John was a priest comes from Polycrates, who was bishop of Ephesus (the city where John spent the last part of his life) towards the end of the second century. His statement, quoted by Eusebius,[18] that John 'was a priest' has been variously interpreted, but it could well be a genuine fragment of literal history. Some slight confirmation of this is provided by the fact that his mother Salome may have had some priestly blood in her veins, since she and her sister Mary were related to Elizabeth, who was 'of the daughters of Aaron'.[19] It was considered desirable, though not obligatory, that priests should take wives from the Aaronic line. So, if John's father Zebedee was a priest, Salome would have been a suitable wife for him. These two items of evidence do not add up to a decisive case, but there seems more than a possibility that John was known to the high priest as an occasional officiant in the temple.[20]

This in itself, however, would not account for John having a home in Jerusalem, or for being well known to the high priest's servants, or indeed of his being 'known' to the high priest except in a quite casual and superficial sense. There is another possibility which would provide a complete explanation. This is how Ronald Brownrigg puts it:

> There was a vast demand for fresh fish and consequently a thriving fishing industry on the lake. Fish were also pickled or cured at Tarichae, Capernaum and other centres, then packed in barrels to be transported by camel and donkey to Jerusalem and Samaria. Quantities of fish would be needed at the great feasts by the multitudes of pilgrims to the temple. Consequently the larger fishing concerns would have their own offices and representatives in Jerusalem .... The fishermen disciples of Jesus were far from all being poor, simple, rustic peasants. Zebedee and his family were of some

substance and status, of considerable skill and business acumen. He employed a hired crew and had at least one sizeable smack for deep-sea fishing ... A particularly interesting possibility is that the firm of 'Zebedee and sons, of Galilee' was contracted to supply fish to the high priest's palace in Jerusalem.[21]

In support of this is an exceptionally interesting quotation from *The Gospel of the Nazareans*, which is found in a fourteenth-century German manuscript. We possess only quoted fragments of this gospel, but it appears to have been a sober book, written in the first half of the second century for orthodox Syrian Jewish Christians, and to be closely related to the Gospel of Matthew. The manuscript reads:

> In the Gospel of the Nazaraeans the reason is given why John was known to the high priest. As he was the son of the poor fisherman Zebedee, he had often brought fish to the palace of the high priests Annas and Caiaphas.[22]

We do not of course know whether this quotation has been correctly transmitted across twelve centuries, and we obviously cannot be sure that *The Gospel of the Nazaraeans* had accurate information — it could be someone's guess at how John got access to the high priestly circle. But it is at any rate an *early, written* tradition from orthodox Christians, and there are a number of things to be said in its favour. (1) It is quite precise in naming a second century book which was not well known in the church at large. (2) It cites a tradition which does not appear to have been known in the church at large.[23] (3) It is not represented as a speculative deduction, but as an illuminating quotation. (4) The tradition itself has intrinsic plausibility.

These two possibilities, that John was known to the high priest both through his occasional temple duties and through his regular business connection, add up to a satisfying explanation of the facts as presented in the gospels.

Other actors, whose identities present fewer problems, will be dealt with in due course as the story unfolds.

CHAPTER FOUR

The Five Writers

Having done our best to throw light upon the more obscure
actors in this drama, it now only remains to say a word or two
about the standpoint and aims of the writers through whom the
story has come to us. One of the most striking things about them
all is their selectivity. None of them attempts to tell the whole
story; all would echo John's closing words: "There are also many
other things which Jesus did; were every one of them to be
written, I suppose that the world itself could not contain the
books that would be written." Each of them ruthlessly selects the
details which serve his purpose.

MATTHEW

The Author's Identity and Aims

Early Christian writers are unanimous that the first gospel was
written by Matthew (otherwise called Levi), the Capernaum
tax-collector who became one of Jesus' twelve apostles. They are
also unanimous that he wrote it in the 'Hebrew' language and
that it was the first to be written. Although most modern scholars
have rejected all this, many are prepared to concede that
Matthew may to some extent have influenced the form which this

gospel took. It will be found that the hypothesis that the gospel was written from Matthew's point of view, and at a time when the Jerusalem church was suffering persecution, throws interesting light on a number of details in the story.

The author appears to have three primary concerns in the last twenty verses of his book. One is to counter the false story circulating in Jerusalem about the disappearance of Jesus' body. It was being said that the disciples came and stole it. He counters this by telling a story which on the face of it takes some believing: Pilate providing a guard for the chief priests, an earthquake, a dazzling angel, soldiers reporting to the chief priests, bribes to tell a tale of sleep while on duty. Such an improbable story (at whatever date it was written down) seems totally useless as apologetic unless those involved knew it to be undeniably true.

His second concern is to tell of the experiences of the Galilean women. More than 200 years ago J.J. Griesbach expressed the view that Matthew's chief informant was Mary, wife of Clopas — 'the other Mary' of this narrative.[1] As we have seen, Clopas appears to have been a brother of Joseph of Nazareth — which would account for Matthew's knowledge of Joseph's side of the infancy story. The other Mary's involvement can also account for the particular slant of his narrative here.

His third concern is to express with great conciseness the terms of the momentous recommissioning on the mountain in Galilee.

Matthew's Whereabouts

A good deal of light would be thrown on Matthew's standpoint if we could establish his physical whereabouts over the period from Thursday night to Sunday morning. We know something of the movements of the apostles on the night of Jesus' arrest in Gethsemane. All of them at first forsook him and fled,[2] though later that night we find Peter and John in the house of the high priest.[3] John had quarters inside the city — the home to which he took the mother of Jesus on Friday afternoon[4] and from which he set off for the tomb with Peter on Sunday morning.[5] So presumably these two had recovered their nerve, re-entered the city and stayed there over this period.

But what of the other nine? We know that in the early part of Holy Week Jesus and his disciples had gone out in the evening to Bethany and had spent the night there.[6] Bethany was nearly two miles from the city on the route that passes the generally accepted site of the Garden of Gethsemane, to which Jesus and the eleven had retired after the Last Supper.[7] When the arresting party arrived from the city their obvious line of retreat was to Bethany. So we may assume that they all set off in that direction. Evidently Peter and John thought better of it and decided to mingle with the crowd returning to the city, but Matthew and the others presumably lay low in or near that village on Good Friday and over the sabbath.

MARK

The Ending of the Gospel

In the case of Mark's gospel we are confronted at once with a major critical question. Where does the gospel end? Although the vast majority of manuscripts end the final chapter at verse 20, there are important manuscripts which end at verse 8, and nearly all scholars in recent years have regarded the last twelve verses as an addition composed considerably later, neither written nor authorised by Mark. Nevertheless, if the gospel does end with the words: "They said nothing to anyone, for they were afraid", there are great difficulties in explaining such an abrupt conclusion and such an apparently negative end to "The Good News of Jesus Christ". Some have argued that the abrupt end is in keeping with Mark's abrupt beginning and that it is a highly dramatic (if indirect) way of announcing the resurrection — the women are speechless with awe at the empty tomb and the angel's message. This seems to be too sophisticated for Mark's down-to-earth gospel, and it is difficult to believe that he did not intend to go on to tell of Jesus' appearance. Some think that Mark had the ill-luck to die or to be forced to flee for his life before he was able to finish his book. But in this case one would expect those who knew his mind and had the custody of his manuscript to have completed it before allowing its publication. Some think that the ending was lost or destroyed by mischance or that it was deliberately suppressed. But in either case the damage would have had to have been done near to the time of publication, if we are to account for the fact that all lines of transmission of the original manuscript were destroyed. But if the loss occurred so early, one would have expected those responsible for publication to have produced new, undamaged copies in order to perpetuate the true tradition.

In spite of the formidable difficulties, however, there has long been a scholarly consensus that Mark's work ends at verse 8 and that verses 9–20 are by a different hand. But this consensus has recently been sharply challenged by W.R. Farmer[8] and it seems wisest to take seriously the possibility that verse 20 might after all be the true end. If the gospel ends at verse 8, it has a few small points to contribute to the overall story, but it presents no problem of gospel harmony. Should it, on the other hand, extend to verse 20 it would (as we shall see in chapter 9) pose an apparently flat contradiction to Luke. In view of the fact that the last twelve verses are in any case an early witness and that they were accepted by the church to be read with the gospel, they have a standing above any of the clearly uncanonical writings. It seems right then to give them serious consideration, instead of taking the easy way of leaving them out of account.

Mark's Aim

If the gospel ends at verse 8 Mark's aim in his final section is to give a dramatic announcement of the resurrection. If verse 20 is the end, Mark's principal concerns would appear to be (1) to highlight the fact that the followers of Jesus were the reverse of credulous, showing persistent unbelief. (2) To stress the fact that these faithless followers had been given a worldwide commission and a promise of divine power for the task. It is these aims which govern his selection of material. There is a strong tradition that Mark worked alongside Peter in Rome and that his gospel is substantially a record of Peter's teaching while there. If this is true, these two themes would of course have been of great interest to them in their missionary work together. We have one detail in the earlier part of the narrative suggesting the apostle's own recollection — the injunction to the women, "Tell his disciples *and Peter*", which is mentioned in no other gospel.

Furthermore, as we shall see, Peter was almost certainly in John's house from early Friday morning till early Sunday morning. We shall see that Mark's account of events over that period seems to be written from the point of view of Peter living there. The women he names at the cross and as buying the spices are precisely the women we have reason to believe were lodging at John's house. In the longer ending we have the appearance to Mary Magdalene. She would obviously have returned to John's house and there told her story to those who 'mourned and wept' (a particularly apt description of Peter). We then have a brief mention of the appearance to Clopas, another of those at John's house, and then an account of the appearance to the Eleven (which included Peter).

Mark's Place in the Story

It would be wrong to suppose that Mark allowed no place to his own observations and individuality in his writing, especially in events in which he played a part. The incident in the Garden of Gethsemane, when the young man who was seized at the time of Jesus' arrest ran away naked leaving his sheet in his captors' hands, has traditionally (and plausibly) been regarded as Mark's own signature to his book.[9] This provides a useful point of introduction from which to investigate Mark's place in the gospel story and it raises the interesting question of why he was in the garden. It has been suggested that the garden belonged to Mark's father. The case for this is by no means negligible, for it can be shown that Mark's home played an important role in the life of the early church, and that the role almost certainly began before Pentecost.

The first point to notice is that the Christians seem to have had access to at least one large meeting-place in Jerusalem from the time of the Last Supper to the time of Peter's escape from prison nearly a decade later, as the following facts show. On Maundy Thursday thirteen of them met in 'a large upper room'.[10] On Easter Sunday evening a somewhat larger group met in a house in Jerusalem well known to Cleopas and his companion.[11] A month or so later 120 people gathered in solemn conclave, evidently in '*the* upper room'.[12] A few days later, on the Day of Pentecost, they were in a house outside which thousands could collect.[13] (This suggests a well-to-do home, since the houses were mostly packed close together within the walled city.) Several years later 'many' were gathered together to pray for Peter's release in what is specifically described as the house of Mary, mother of John Mark.[14] It seems rather unlikely that the persecuted followers of Jesus had more than one really large place of meeting in the city, so we may conclude that all these gatherings probably took place in Mark's home.

The second point to notice is that such commitment to the cause of Jesus by a wealthy citizen at a time when the Galilean's fortunes were at their lowest ebb was a remarkable phenomenon, in striking contrast to the secret discipleship of Joseph of Arimathea and Nicodemus. Its roots must surely reach back to an earlier period. Mark's father must have known Jesus and welcomed him to his home during earlier visits to the city. In view of the official hostility to Jesus, it seems rather unlikely that there was anyone else of comparable standing with comparable commitment in Jerusalem. We do know, however, that there was an unnamed wealthy benefactor who for some time had put his garden at Jesus' disposal, and that Jesus had 'often met there with his disciples'.[15] The garden was evidently a place where Jesus and his disciples could find privacy even during the great festivals, when the city and neighbourhood were teeming with people. It would therefore have had high walls and a door that could be secured.[16] It seems quite possible therefore that we have here an earlier glimpse of Mark's father. If, in addition, we are right in believing that the young man in the garden was Mark, we have a further reason for thinking that this may be so, and the possibility becomes a probability. In the early days when these stories were first told and members of the Jerusalem church were suffering persecution, it would not be surprising to find neither the owner of the upper room nor the owner of Gethsemane identified by name.

Two possible reasons may be suggested for Mark being in the garden. Possibly Judas had brought the arresting party back to the scene of the Last Supper, and Mark, roused from sleep, having heard their errand, had thrown a sheet round him and raced down the mile or so to Gethsemane to raise the alarm. But it was a long way to go so scantily attired and it might not have been so easy to have slipped away unobserved in the light of the

Paschal full moon. Furthermore, John stresses that Judas knew the garden and seems most naturally to imply that he went straight there.[17]

The other possibility is that Mark's hospitable home had a houseful of passover visitors and that it had been arranged that some should spend the night at the other family property. It seems likely that when making arrangements for the meal with his disciples, Jesus would also as a matter of course have made arrangements with his host for the night (even though he himself knew that none of them would sleep the night through). It would have been fitting for Mark, as the young man of the house, if he (together with the disciples of Jesus) had made room for others by going to sleep in one of the buildings of the family oliveyard. During Jesus' long agony in the garden outside Mark would doubtless have been sound asleep, only to be wakened by the crowd battering at the gate.

The location of Mark's home throws light on one feature of his account. Although he knew of Jesus' promised appearance in Galilee,[18] he confines his record to happenings in and around Jerusalem. This might be explained by the fact that he himself did not go north with the Galileans, but stayed in his home city up to the time of the Ascension. What distinguishes him so sharply from Matthew is the fact that he is not concerned to rebut the story of the stolen body, so says nothing about the guard.

LUKE

Though Luke is the most prolific writer in the New Testament and the author of two of the greatest works ever written, he is an elusive figure. Apart from a handful of casual references in Paul's letters and three sections of Acts which are written in the first person plural (so showing his presence, but saying nothing about him personally), the New Testament gives no information about his character or his doings. But tradition is consistent that Luke, the Beloved Physician of the Colossian letter[19] and the travel companion of Paul, was author of the third gospel and of Acts.

The content of Luke's resurrection story is quite different from that of Matthew and Mark, with new persons named and new incidents recorded. The mention of Joanna among the

women going to the tomb and of Cleopas as one of the two going
to Emmaus seem to provide the key to Luke's particular
viewpoint — the visit to the tomb being written from Joanna's
angle and the two subsequent appearances in Emmaus and
Jerusalem being from the angle of Cleopas and his companion.
This Joanna (as we have seen) was wife of one of Herod's senior
officials, named Chuza. That she was probably Luke's informant
is borne out by the fact that Luke shows himself particularly
well-informed about Herod's affairs, including his unique
account of Jesus' interview with Herod on Good Friday
morning.[20]

Luke has three aims, all of which are relevant to the missionary task in which he and Paul had been engaged. Firstly, he aims
to present the historical facts, showing how the unbelieving
followers of Jesus came to believe. In this he emphasises the
physical nature of the resurrection, describing the Jesus of flesh
and bones, who ate fish in their presence. Secondly, he stresses
the fulfilment of Old Testament prophecy. Thirdly, he presents
the message of Christ in his sufferings and exaltation which is to
be preached in the power of the Spirit to all nations for the
forgiveness of sins.

JOHN

The early Christian writers are unanimous that the author of
the fourth gospel was John the apostle, who spent the last part of
his life in Ephesus. Although this testimony has been widely
rejected in modern times, it is still reasonable to believe that the
apostle was at least in some way behind it.[21]

The overall aim of the gospel is made clear at 20:31 — it is to
provide a basis for the life-giving faith which comes through
believing that Jesus is the Son of God. There is stress on the
historical trustworthiness of what is written and thus on the
manhood of Jesus — in our narratives he is the one who could be
touched, the one who cooked breakfast for his disciples — and
there is stress on the unique Sonship of Jesus, whom the gospel
introduces as God the Word and who in the great climax of
chapter 20 is confessed by Thomas as 'My Lord and my God!' In
chapter 21 there is a subsidiary aim, to counter the rumour that
Jesus had said that John would not die. The evangelist rebuts the

story by an accurate recollection of what Jesus had actually said. This indeed seems to be his intention throughout — he uses carefully stored memories to supplement the records of the other evangelists:[22] John was at the cross, he took the Lord's mother to his own home in Jerusalem, he saw the piercing of Jesus' side, he heard Mary Magdalene's report of the removed gravestone, he himself ran to the tomb and experienced the first beginnings of renewed faith, he was present at three successive revelations of Jesus, he heard the Lord's threefold injunction to Peter to feed his flock.

PAUL

Paul's short contribution can be quoted in full:

> For I delivered to you as of first importance what I also received, that Christ died for our sins in accordance with the scriptures, that he was buried, that he was raised on the third day in accordance with the scriptures, and that he appeared to Cephas, then to the twelve. Then he appeared to more than five hundred brethren at one time, most of whom are still alive, though some have fallen asleep. Then he appeared to James, then to all the apostles. Last of all, as to one untimely born, he appeared also to me.
>
> (*1 Corinthians 15:3–8*)

The authenticity of Paul's First Letter to the Corinthians has seldom been doubted even by very sceptical scholars. It was sent from Ephesus probably in the spring of AD 54, and so is usually held to antedate the gospels by one or more decades, and its treatment of the resurrection is thus regarded as of particular importance. The apostle's aim in the fifteenth chapter is to remind his readers of the historical basis on which the gospel stands, as a prelude to a discussion of the resurrection of Christian believers.

Paul, it will be noticed, makes no reference to the empty tomb and gives no account of appearances of Jesus to the women. Furthermore he ends his list of appearances by referring to his own vision of Jesus. On the strength of this experience it has been argued (a) that Paul's encounter with Jesus was not physical, but purely spiritual; (b) that all the other supposed encounters of disciples with the risen Christ were spiritual, not physical; (c) that stories of the empty tomb, of angelic messages and of physical contacts with Jesus were tales that had grown up in the Christian community as Christians tried to give concrete form to their vivid realisation that their crucified Lord was alive and present among them.

Of course none of this is necessary even on the supposition of the late dates usually ascribed to the gospels. True recollections could very well have been preserved for many decades either through careful oral transmission or in the form of written memoirs which were incorporated into the gospels at the time of their composition. The early Christians certainly believed that the gospels were trustworthy records, and there is no reason to think that they were so gullible and uncritical that they would regard the tales of story-tellers as authoritative and canonical. Indeed the treatment which they meted out to the apocryphal gospels shows just the opposite. The evangelists stress that the early witnesses saw him with their eyes, heard with their ears, handled him with their hands, and ate and drank with him.[23]

Paul's contribution is of particular value for the latter part of the resurrection story. The early part of the story necessitates the intricate interweaving of four overlapping, but largely[24] independent, accounts. The difficulties of the latter part are not due to overlapping, but to intense compression. John and Acts both stress that much is left out.[25] Part of the greatness of all the evangelists lies in this ability to confine themselves to what serves their purpose and to omit a multitude of details and qualifications irrelevant to that purpose, no matter how important they may be in other connections. For instance, it is unthinkable that Luke, who knew Paul's teaching about the resurrection and who himself was to state in Acts that Jesus appeared during forty days, could have supposed (or intended his readers to suppose) that the events between the resurrection and the ascension were crowded into one day, even though his account could be read that way. These writers are not attempting a leisurely account of the whole history. They are more like advocates in a court of law, with limited time and space, trying to summon the most telling evidence. Paul's pithy contribution is invaluable in linking up the brief accounts of the evangelists.

We should particularly note his opening words: "I delivered to you as of first importance what I also received." Paul claims that the tradition which he had handed on to the Corinthians with such emphasis and authority was a tradition which he had received from those who held authority before him. This must mean from the apostolic circle, and presumably refers to instruction which he received in Jerusalem not long after his conversion perhaps no more than five years after the crucifixion (see Galatians 1:18f). Some scholars argue that the wording of the list suggests that he had acquired a written formula. Be that as it may, Paul has made the list his own. He does not intend it to be exhaustive, for he does not mention (or at least clearly identify) any of the incidents which his travel-companion and 'biographer' Luke records — the visit of the women to the tomb, the Emmaus appearance or its sequels in Jerusalem and on the way to Bethany. He seems to present a list of Christ's revelations to his officially commissioned representatives. His failure to mention the women is not surprising, since in Jewish law a woman's witness was not readily accepted in court.[26] But Cleopas and his companion also had no official status and their meeting with Jesus was not a recommissioning.[27]

It is true that Paul makes no explicit mention of the empty tomb, but he goes out of his way to say that Jesus not only died, but 'that he was buried'. In mainline Judaism resurrection was nothing if not resurrection of the body. So in mentioning the burial, he is calling attention to what happened to the body — it was consigned to a burial place, it was raised on the third day and it was seen by a series of people afterwards. An empty tomb is implied.[28] Further, to say 'that he was raised on the third day' would make no sense if Paul was thinking of spiritual survival in spite of bodily death, since Jesus could be said to have survived death from the moment of expiry. This 'third day' motif, it should be noted, occurs eleven times in the New Testament. A striking illustration of the public recognition of the empty tomb can be seen in Peter's Pentecost sermon and in Paul's sermon at Antioch.[29] Peter calls attention to the nearby tomb of David in which that patriarch's body suffered corruption. Christ by contrast, he asserts, was resurrected and his flesh did not see corruption. Paul similarly says that David saw corruption, whereas Jesus did not.

Paul's repeated 'then ... then ... then ... then ... last of all' seems most naturally to indicate that the order is chronological. Some have suggested that the arrangement might be schematic,

but it is difficult to see any convincing scheme in the arrangement: Cephas, Twelve, 500, James, all the apostles, Paul. If we
work on the assumption that the order is chronological, it is
possible (as we shall see) fairly confidently to equate some of
these appearances with appearances in the gospels.

Armed now with some knowledge of the place and of the
people and with some understanding of the viewpoints of our five
writers, we can begin to trace out the Easter story — not of
course with any infallibility of detail, but with some assurance as
to its main particulars. We shall first sketch in the events which
brought Jesus to the cross and then we shall examine the records
of the subsequent happenings in detail. Throughout, it must be
realised, we shall be concerned with historical probabilities based
upon the conclusions reached so far, but we shall try not to weary
the reader with endless "probablys". These must be taken as
read.

CHAPTER 5

Good Friday

THE MAN THEY CRUCIFIED

Jesus was a strange and wonderful man. For more than three years he had been the talk of Palestine. All agreed that he was a magnetic personality with astonishing powers of healing. It was common knowledge that for hours at a time he could hold great crowds spellbound as he talked. By his goodness and power he had attracted an enormous following of men and women from all walks of life. Yet to everyone he had presented an enigma.

Never once had he publicly either asserted or denied that he was the Messiah, yet he had repeatedly said and done things which not only implied Messiahship, but even implied divinity.[1] On one occasion his seeming equivocation had so exasperated his hearers that they said to him, "How long will you keep us in suspense? If you are the Christ, tell us plainly."[2] But his reply had only exasperated them further. Though some of his admirers had come to think of him as Messiah at a very early stage,[3] Jesus did not explicitly confirm their belief for a long time. He allowed them long experience both of his love and power and also of his rejection by a growing number of influential people before he declared himself. And even then, when at last in the privacy of his withdrawal to Caesarea Philippi he confirmed Peter's declaration, "You are the Christ, the Son of the Living God," he had chilled their enthusiasm by solemnly forbidding his disciples to repeat what he had said in public.[4]

His assertion of Messiahship had in fact done little to clear the confusion in the disciples' minds, because he had at once proceeded to follow it up with prophecies of his coming sufferings and crucifixion. His concept of Messiahship was so alien to all their thoughts that they had been incapable of taking it in. Jesus himself, however, had been fully aware of his unique relation to the Father right from the beginning of his ministry, and he had been aware that his ministry was to be one of conquest through suffering. His role was to be that of the Suffering Servant spoken of by the prophet Isaiah and of the Smitten Shepherd spoken of by the prophet Zechariah.[5]

Now he had come to Jerusalem for the last time to present himself to Israel as their king — but as a very strange sort of king. On the Sunday, accompanied by crowds of Galilean pilgrims shouting and waving palm branches, he acted out the prophecy of Zechariah, which said,

> Rejoice greatly, O daughter of Zion!
> Shout aloud, O daughter of Jerusalem!
> Lo, your king comes to you;
>   triumphant and victorious is he,
> humble and riding on an ass,
>   on a colt the foal of an ass.[6]

When Thursday came his behaviour was stranger than ever. While eating the Passover meal with the disciples he spoke of his coming death as an atoning sacrifice for the forgiveness of the sins of men.[7] Then he prayed aloud, revealing to their dazed minds his inner communion with Father and Spirit, and he spoke of his eternal purposes for them and for those who would one day come to believe through them.[8]

THE SMITTEN SHEPHERD

Now the hour had come to face the final agony. When they had sung a psalm, Jesus led his disciples from the upper room; they passed out through one of the city gates, and went across the Kidron valley to the foot of the Mount of Olives. On the way he

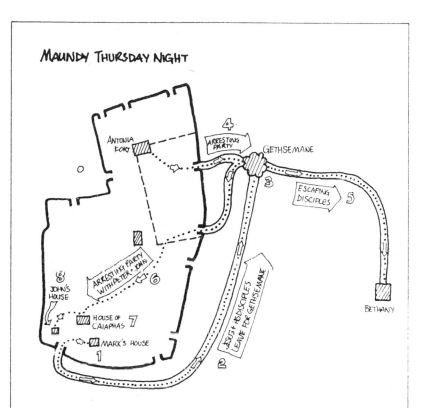

MAUNDY THURSDAY NIGHT

1. Jesus eats the Passover with the twelve in Mark's house. Judas leaves to arrange his arrest.
2. Jesus, the Eleven and Mark leave the house and cross the Kidron Valley. Jesus warns them that the Shepherd will be struck down and the sheep scattered.
3. They enter Gethsemane, where Jesus prays.
4. Judas arrives with an arresting party, consisting of members of the Temple guard and soldiers from the Roman garrison, stationed at the Antonia Fort to the north of the Temple.
5. The Eleven escape up the Mount of Olives in the direction of Bethany; Mark is nearly caught.
6. Jesus is taken back to the city; Peter and John think better of their cowardice and join the returning company, which goes to the high priest's residence. At the house of Caiaphas, Peter denies Jesus.
7. John takes Peter to his home, where Zebedee and Salome, Clopas and Mary, and Jesus' Mother await them.

warned them that in accordance with God's foreordained purposes they would that night desert him. "For it is written," he
said, quoting Zechariah, "'I will strike the shepherd, and the
sheep of the flock will be scattered,' but after I am raised up, I
will go before you to Galilee."[9] All of them, and Peter in
particular, declared with vehemence that they would never
disown him.

Jesus then led them, as he had so often done before, into the
Garden of Gethsemane, which had been placed at his disposal by
its kindly owner, John Mark's father, who was a well-to-do
Jerusalem citizen. It was not just an ornamental garden, but it
contained an olive grove and an oil-press and farm buildings,
where Mark and others of his over-crowded household could
sleep on that chilly April night. It was surrounded by a high wall
to protect it from the hungry populace of Jerusalem. Taking
Peter, James and John with him, Jesus left the other eight
disciples and went to another part of the garden to pray. As he
prayed long in agony, submitting himself wholly to his Father's
will, his weary supporters fell asleep.

Then suddenly came a violent knocking at the gate. Someone
opened the door to see Judas standing there, backed by a motley
crowd of servants of the high priest carrying torches and armed
with swords and cudgels, and in the background a contingent of
Roman soldiers under the command of their chiliarch.[10] Jesus
went out to them. The sight of his imposing figure, awesome in
spiritual power, struck them with fear and they moved back,
falling over one another in disarray.

The disciples emerged from the garden behind Jesus and a
scuffle ensued, during which Peter drew a sword and cut off the
right ear of one of the high priest's slaves called Malchus. At this
critical moment of his self-surrender Jesus did his last miracle of
healing — he restored the man's ear. He then spoke calmly to the
arresting party, making it clear that he was about to give himself
voluntarily to their power. He demanded that his disciples
should be allowed to leave, at which the eleven made their
escape. Mark, however, was nearly caught. Awakened by the
arresting party, he had thrown a sheet round him, and kept close
to Jesus even while the others were effecting their get-away.
Then someone had spotted him and tried to seize him; he let go

of the sheet and fled, leaving the impromptu garment in the man's hand.

THE SCATTERED SHEEP

The obvious line of retreat for the apostles was in the opposite direction to that by which Judas and his company had come; that is, away from Jerusalem up the familiar rough track which led from the Kidron valley over the Mount of Olives in the direction of Bethany, where Lazarus, Martha and Mary Magdalene lived. John and Peter soon thought better of their desertion, and took the risk of joining the hangers-on who were returning to the city with the arresting party. But the other nine, when removed by a safe distance, looked down on the city and saw with perfect clearness the lights of the torches passing through the city gateway. They went back to Bethany in distress and fear, believing that not only Jesus, but also John and Peter, were under arrest.

John and Peter meanwhile had been able, because of the former's knowledge of the high priest and his servants, to gain access to the house of Caiaphas. There Peter witnessed his Master's bold confession. In response to the solemn adjuration of Caiaphas, "Are you the Christ, the Son of the Blessed One?" Jesus replied for the first time in public, "I am."[11] Peter himself, all his resistance gone in the chill night air of the courtyard, was challenged by the mocking taunt of the servant girl and the relentless probing of a slave, and he found himself disowning his Master with oaths and curses. The Lord turned and looked at Peter, and Peter went out and wept bitterly.

John took Peter in all his misery to his own house at which his parents and various relatives were staying for the festival. He broke the news of Jesus' arrest to them — to the Lord's mother, to his parents Zebedee and Salome and to Clopas and to Clopas' wife Mary — all of whose minds had been filled with anxious forebodings. The night passed and Good Friday dawned. As the terrible day proceeded on its fateful course these three women, supported presumably by the two husbands and by John himself, went out into the city and followed through the grim events. Peter, distraught, broken by shame, unable to trust himself not to disgrace his name further in the dangers outside, hid behind closed doors in hopeless dejection.

The disciples at Bethany remained in acute apprehension, knowing nothing of what had happened to their comrades and far too frightened to show their faces in Jerusalem. Though feeling reasonably safe at Bethany, knowing that the authorities would hardly trouble to seek them out so far away at such a busy time, they were nonetheless anxious about their friends and also about the three mothers in the city. The devoted Mary Magdalene was the obvious one to go to Jerusalem to find out what had happened, and she soon joined her friends at the Place of a Skull.

AT THE CROSS

From this point in the story we need to follow our four evangelists in greater detail. According to Mark the crucifixion lasted from the third to the ninth hour.[12] John recalls two incidents which apparently took place at the beginning of this period: the dividing of Jesus' clothes among the four soldiers and the committing of Jesus' mother to his care. Of the latter he says:

> Standing by the cross of Jesus were his mother, and his mother's sister, Mary the wife of Clopas, and Mary Magdalene. When Jesus saw his mother, and the disciple whom he loved standing near, he said to his mother, 'Woman, behold your son!' Then he said to the disciple, 'Behold your mother!' And from that hour the disciple took her to his own home.[13]

The other three evangelists do not mention the presence of the women till after Jesus has died, though they imply in general terms that they had watched what had gone on. Both Matthew and Mark speak of many women, among whom three are specially identified, while Luke adds that men were also present: 'all his (male) acquaintances'.[14] This expression can be used of either acquaintances or relatives. Both were probably there. It is remarkable that Luke avoids the term 'disciples', which seems to confirm our deduction that the nine were in hiding in Bethany. We have already inferred the presence of two male relatives:

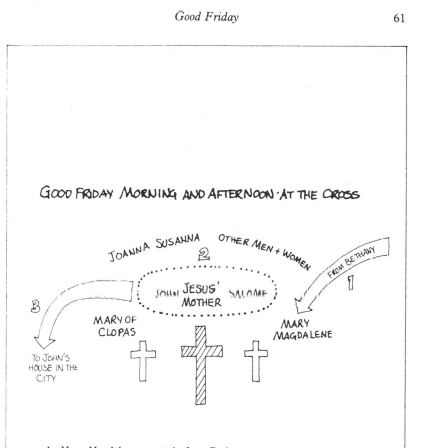

GOOD FRIDAY MORNING AND AFTERNOON · AT THE CROSS

1. Mary Magdalene comes in from Bethany.
2. The Lord's Mother, Mary Magdalene, Mary of Clopas, Salome and Salome's son, John, come near to the cross; other relatives and well-wishers (including Joanna and 'Susanna') stand further back.
3. John and Salome take the Lord's Mother to their home in the city.

After the Lord's death, Joseph of Arimathea gets permission to bury Jesus, and the body is taken to his tomb.
Joseph buys the great cloth and Nicodemus the spices.

Zebedee, Salome's husband and Clopas, the husband of the other Mary. In mentioning male acquaintances Luke mitigates the otherwise unrelieved baseness of the men, as he does also by pointing out that Joseph was a good man, who had not consented to the decision of the Sanhedrin.

All three evangelists speak of these men and women as watching from a distance, and might seem to imply that they were there at the end, though (as we shall see in a moment) Salome did not remain throughout — which shows the danger of reading into an author's words more than he actually says. John's account of the four women standing near the cross seems to be an incident near the beginning of the agony. Jesus' mother, supported by her nephew John and accompanied by Mary Magdalene, Salome and Mary of Clopas, was evidently allowed by the centurion to come close to the cross for a while. This man showed his sympathies later on, when the cry of awe was wrung from him and his companions, "Certainly this man was Son of God."[15]

Jesus now commits his mother to the care of the beloved disciple: "He said to the disciple, 'Behold your mother!'" An apparently undesigned coincidence[16] may be seen here in the fact that John had happened to remark at an earlier stage that Jesus' brothers "did not believe in him".[17] This may in part explain why they could not comfort their mother in her distress, though it is also probable that they (like the nine disciples) had in fact fled the city. Luke, however, mentions that after the ascension a change had come over them — both his mother and his brothers devoted themselves to prayer with the eleven as they awaited the baptism of the Holy Spirit.[18] But at this stage his brothers were still unbelieving. John says: "From that hour the disciple took her to his own home." There is no mention of Salome going, but it is natural that the Virgin Mary's sister (who was also John's mother) should have gone too. This (as we shall see) fits the unexplained disappearance of Salome in Matthew's and Mark's accounts of the burial — another good example of an undesigned coincidence, this time corroborating both the Johannine and the Synoptic accounts.

There follows a gap in John's narrative of some hours, which suggests that he stayed with his new mother for a considerable time before returning to witness the end. He then heard the

Lord's "I thirst" and "It is finished" and his final yielding up of his spirit. All this happened on 'the day of Preparation' which as Mark explains[19] simply means Friday, the day before the Sabbath. The Jewish authorities, therefore, anxious that the bodies should not remain on the cross on the holy day asked Pilate that the legs of those crucified should be broken. (It was part of the crucifixion torture that the crucified man needed the support of his legs if he was continually to keep raising himself sufficiently to keep breathing.)[20] John saw this despatching of the two criminals by the soldiers and then witnessed how they came to Jesus and saw that he was already dead, they did not break his legs. But one of the soldiers pierced his side with a spear, and at once there came out blood and water.

Although Joanna, by reason of her position in Herod's court, stood slightly apart from the trio of watching women to whom we have referred, it is probable that she was one of the 'many' others who were there at least part of the time, and (as we shall see) was probably there at the end. Among other male 'acquaintances' likely to have been present were Joseph of Arimathea and Nicodemus, who were to figure prominently in the next series of events.

Joseph is described as a rich man, a respected member of the Sanhedrin, who had not consented to their decision and action against Jesus, a good man who was looking for the kingdom of God. A shocking realisation must have suddenly come over Joseph and the other well-wishers of Jesus. They realised that the body of Jesus would shortly be hauled down and thrown into the common criminals' grave along with the corpses of the two thieves. Joseph of Arimathea, hitherto according to John a secret disciple of Jesus, found himself confronted by a momentous decision. His own garden, right by the place of crucifixion, had a newly-cut, unused tomb in which Jesus could easily be buried. Dare he openly declare his discipleship and ask for the custody of the body? A kindly providence forced his hand — he must act now or not at all. According to Mark he plucked up courage and went direct to the governor to seek his permission. This must have been in the late afternoon at about the time of the waving of the first-fruits, an important ceremony in the Passover season at which the chief priests would probably have been present.[21] This could account for the fact that Joseph met with no opposition from them when he made his request, which the governor granted forthwith.

THE BURIAL

Four people are named as being present at the burial. All the evangelists mention Joseph; Matthew and Mark mention Mary Magdalene and the other Mary as "sitting opposite the sepulchre",[22] seeing "*where* he was laid". (No mention, notice, of the other member of the trio, Salome, who had gone with her sister, Jesus' mother, to John's home.) John adds Nicodemus. Luke, too, adds to our information, but indirectly. He is in one respect less specific: he says, "The women who had come with him from Galilee followed," perhaps aware that the mention of the two Marys was not the whole story. In another respect he is more specific: he says that the women followed Joseph who had gone into the tomb and they saw "*how* his body was laid." The outside view of *where* he was laid and this inside view of *how* he was laid is very suggestive. It ties in with what Luke is shortly going to tell us about the women who returned to the grave on Sunday morning. He mentions Mary Magdalene, Mary the mother of James, Joanna and *other women* (in the plural). One of the other women was, we know, Salome, but this still leaves at least one unnamed woman to account for. It is tempting to think of her as the well-to-do Susanna who is linked with Joanna at Luke 8:3, though there is no means of verifying the guess. Joanna, a member of Herod's court, would probably have been on easy terms with Joseph, the prominent Sanhedrist, so it seems likely that she (and perhaps her friend 'Susanna') followed Joseph into the tomb and helped to lay out the body, while the Marys watched at a respectful distance. The Nicodemus whom John mentions was, like Joseph, a distinguished member of the Sanhedrin and like him was also a secret disciple. He had once visited Jesus by night, possibly in John's house, and had there heard of the need of a new birth.[23]

It thus seems probable that on his return from Pilate Joseph took urgent counsel with Nicodemus and the women about what to do in the short time before nightfall and the onset of the sabbath. In the ordinary way the body would have been washed and anointed with perfumed oils before being dressed in a clean

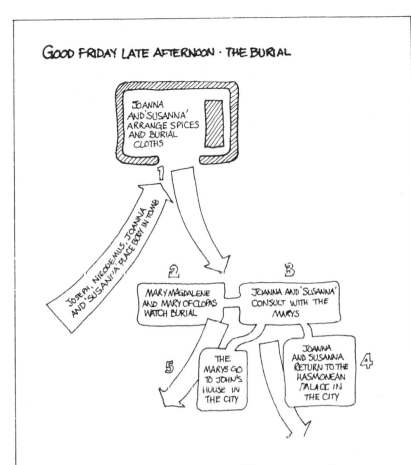

GOOD FRIDAY LATE AFTERNOON · THE BURIAL

1. Joanna and 'Susanna' follow Joseph and his servants and Nicodemus into the tomb to help lay out the body.
2. Meanwhile, the two Marys watch from a distance.
3. The four women confer and agree to return at first light on Sunday to anoint the body.
4. Joanna and 'Susanna' return to the Hasmonean Palace and prepare ointments.
5. Mary of Clopas takes Mary Magdalene to John's house.

outer garment. But there was clearly insufficient time to do all this. So it seems that Joseph agreed to get a large linen cloth from the market to wrap the body in and Nicodemus to get a liberal supply of dry spices to pack round the body to act as a partial anti-putrifacient as a temporary measure, while the women agreed to return to the tomb at the first possible moment after the sabbath was over to anoint the body properly.

The precise nature of the burial cloths has been the subject of much debate. The synoptists tell us that Joseph of Arimathea bought (Mark) a clean (Matthew) linen shroud or sheet (Greek – *sindon*) and wrapped Jesus in it (Matthew, Mark, Luke). John mentions no shroud, but speaks in the plural of linen cloths (*othonia*) and also of a *soudarion* — "the napkin, which had been on his head ... rolled up in a place by itself." The disputed (but probably authentic) passage at Luke 24:12 makes no further reference to the sheet, but mentions *othonia* lying by themselves.

Christian artists have commonly depicted the grave-clothes of Jesus as broad bandages wound round the limbs and the body, together with a turban-like towel around his head. Some writers have visualised the linen sheet being torn into strips and the spices being wound into the folds. It has then been supposed that at the resurrection the *soudarion* and *othonia* collapsed in situ to form two separate piles. As will be seen presently this does not in fact tally very well with what the evangelists say, but it illustrates the apparently rather imprecise and confusing picture which they seem to give.

John gives us an account of a normal burial in a well-to-do home in his record of the raising of Lazarus: "The dead man came out, his hands and feet bound with bandages (*keiriai*), and his face wrapped with a cloth (*soudarion*). Jesus said to them, 'Unbind him, and let him go.'"[24] There is nothing in this account to suggest a winding of long bandages around arms and legs and other parts of the body; indeed just the opposite, for the resuscitated corpse was certainly not deprived of wrappings which left him standing there naked. Before burial he had been washed, anointed with perfumed ointments and dressed in his best clean garment. Short strips of cloth had apparently been tied round wrists and ankles to keep his arms and legs in position, and the *soudarion* kept the mouth from falling open. The hobbled Lazarus was able to shuffle to the entrance of the tomb, where he was set free by the untying of these three cloths. And now he stood there fully clothed.

The burial of Jesus, on the other hand, was most unusual. Everything had to be done under extreme pressure of time before the sabbath began at dusk. There was no time to wash the body, no time to procure ointments and no garment with which to dress the corpse. So Joseph bought his length of cloth and Nicodemus his huge quantity of dry spices (100 litrai is about thirty-three kilogrammes, more than five stone) — lavish provision fit for a king. It is an interesting question whether John himself saw the interment. He was present at the time of Jesus' death and one would imagine that he would be as concerned as anyone to see him decently buried and to be able to tell the Lord's mother that his body had not been cast into a common grave with the criminals. He more than any other disciple would have been likely to know Joseph and Nicodemus. So he may actually have helped Nicodemus carry his great load of spices. He goes on to say, "They bound it in linen cloths with spices, as is the burial custom of the Jews." John here seems to be making a broad distinction between the Jewish custom, which was simply to anoint the body with perfumed oils and to surround it with spices, and the Egyptian custom of disembowelling, embalming and swathing with bandages, or the Roman practice of cremation. Presumably the jaw and wrists and ankles were bound together, the body was wrapped in the great sheet with the spices around it, and the women agreed to return at first light when the sabbath was over to do the anointing as best they could. Before they left they saw Joseph's servants roll the great gravestone against the entrance to the tomb. They departed, Joanna and 'Susanna' to the Hasmonean palace, and the two Marys to John's house, it being by that time too late for Mary Magdalene to return to Bethany.

CHAPTER 6

Saturday

PREPARING THE OINTMENTS

Before the women could return a number of things took place. Matthew, Mark and Luke all provide information, and conjecture adds some further interesting possibilities. Luke (our Joanna source)[1] shows himself virtually, if not entirely, independent of Mark and Matthew. He says the women "returned, and prepared spices and ointments. On the sabbath they rested according to the commandment." Mark, however, says, "When the sabbath was past, Mary Magdalene, and Mary the mother of James, and Salome, bought spices, so that they might go and anoint him." Luke does not actually say that the women prepared the ointments before the sabbath rest, though without evidence to the contrary that is how one would naturally take it.[2] But Mark is quite explicit that they waited till sundown, "when the sabbath was past" and the shops were open once more. It would contradict nothing explicitly said by Luke if we were to infer that the preparation of the spices and ointments to which he refers did in fact take place after their purchase on Saturday evening; it would simply negate an impression. There is, however, an interesting alternative.

Wealthy Jewesses were accustomed to spend large sums on perfumes and ointments[3] and it is quite possible that Joanna and 'Susanna' were able to prepare their share of the burial ointments from their own resources on Friday evening without having recourse to the Saturday market. In that case Luke's is a straightforward account written from Joanna's point of view, whereas Mark's is an account written from the point of view of the other three women who spent their sabbath in John's house. Peter, it will be remembered, had taken refuge there after his denials and was still there on Sunday morning, so Mark is giving us his mentor's point of view. Peter doubtless recalled how Salome had come back on Friday morning, supporting the Lord's mother, and how at nightfall Mary Magdalene and Mary, wife of Clopas, had joined them as the sabbath began.

On that sabbath we reckon that in addition to the four women, there would have been in that house four men: Peter and John and the two husbands, Zebedee and Clopas. For all of them it must have been a night and day of unrelieved gloom, with minds and bodies exhausted. But as the day proceeded two things would increasingly have occupied their thoughts. One was the need to procure the ointments which they had undertaken to bring for the anointing on Sunday morning; the other was the breakdown of communication with the apostles at Bethany, of whom nothing had been heard for nearly two days. It seems probable that they worked out a careful plan ready for the ending of the sabbath; it entailed an expedition to the market and an expedition to Bethany.

Mark is quite explicit that the three women *bought* spices — they did not have the ingredients for the ointments in their possession like the wealthy Joanna. Mary Magdalene was named by Luke (8:2) as among the well-to-do, but on this occasion she needs to procure her share like the Galileans, Salome and Mary wife of Clopas. If it is true that she was the one who used up her most precious ointment upon Jesus at Bethany, we see here another of those small coincidences which abound in these narratives. It is not particularly likely that the women made three separate little purchases, but rather that one of them (perhaps Salome who as an occasional resident in Jerusalem knew the market best) bought on behalf of them all. Indeed a plausible conjecture suggests that the Marys may have been involved in the Bethany expedition at the very time when Salome was buying the spices.

Both Mary Magdalene and the other Mary would have had strong reasons for wanting to get out to Bethany as soon as

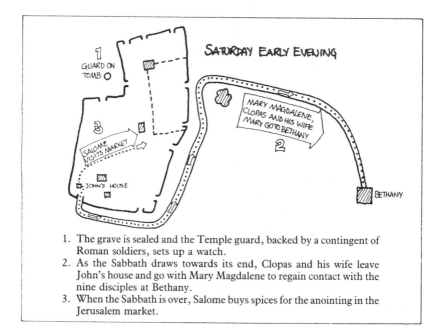

SATURDAY EARLY EVENING

GUARD ON TOMB

MARY MAGDALENE, CLOPAS AND HIS WIFE MARY GO TO BETHANY

SALOME VISITS MARKET

JOHN'S HOUSE

BETHANY

1. The grave is sealed and the Temple guard, backed by a contingent of Roman soldiers, sets up a watch.
2. As the Sabbath draws towards its end, Clopas and his wife leave John's house and go with Mary Magdalene to regain contact with the nine disciples at Bethany.
3. When the Sabbath is over, Salome buys spices for the anointing in the Jerusalem market.

possible — the former because her home and her brother and sister were there, and the latter because she had a son there, James the younger. The first opportunity to do so without breaking the sabbath was on Saturday evening. They could have gone a 'sabbath-day's journey' (say to the crest of Olivet) as the sabbath was ending, and completed the walk down to the village as the stars began to come out, heralding the beginning of the first day of a new Jewish week. Clopas would naturally have accompanied his wife — indeed the onset of darkness would have made his company necessary. Salome also had a son in Bethany, James the elder, but she may well have thought that Jesus' mother had a prior call on her attention, and so they agreed that she should remain in the Zebedee house with the ointments ready to await the return of the others early next morning. When the three arrived at Bethany, they could only confirm to the dejected nine the appalling news that the other residents of Bethany had been bringing in from the city during the past two days. The one ray of comfort they could offer was the knowledge of the safety of Peter and John and of Jesus' mother. (All this is of course only reasoned conjecture, but it is strikingly confirmed in its main point if we are right in thinking that Matthew is describing what happened from the point of view of the nine apostles in Bethany. When he speaks of the departure of the women next morning, he specifically names the two whom we have suggested had particular reason to go to Bethany. For he says "Mary Magdalene and the other Mary went to see the tomb.")[4]

GUARDING THE TOMB

While the women were formulating and executing their plans, (and quite unknown to them) surprising events were taking place in connection with the tomb. Matthew says:

> Next day, that is, after the day of Preparation, the chief priests and the Pharisees gathered before Pilate and said, 'Sir, we remember how that impostor said, while he was still alive, "After three days I will rise again." Therefore order the sepulchre to be made secure until the third day, lest his disciples go and steal him away, and tell the people, "He has risen from the dead," and the last fraud will be worse than the first.' Pilate said to them, 'You have a guard of soldiers; go, make it as secure as you can.' So they went and made the sepulchre secure by sealing the stone and setting a guard.
>
> (*Matthew 27:62–66*)

The placing of the guard was 'next day *after* the day of Preparation', that is, on the day after Friday. In other words, it was on Saturday that the members of the Sanhedrin took such alarm that, even though it was sabbath, they sent a deputation of Pharisees and Sadducees to Pilate. How are we to account for this remarkable move? There are a number of possibilities.

Firstly, the authorities had a deep underlying fear of Jesus. This is one of the most brilliant conclusions of Frank Morison's famous book *Who Moved the Stone?*[5] It was not only that they had feared an uprising by the people, which Jesus could easily have provoked at that time of excitement, but they had feared Jesus' own powers, they feared that he might prove unarrestable. Their decision to arrest him very late on Thursday night was the result of news brought by Judas for which they were unprepared. Judas had brought them news that Jesus was giving himself up. Judas told them that Jesus was ready to accept death and had indeed made it clear that he would remain close at hand in Gethsemane till his captors came. There was something like a three-hour delay between Judas' quitting the supper and the arrival of the arresting party, to be accounted for by momentous discussions among the Jewish authorities and by a crucial interview with Pilate to ensure his swift approval of Jesus' condemnation in the morning. In the event (happily for them) their fears had come to nothing and despite hitches on Pilate's part by nightfall next day their prey was dead. However, the tearing curtain and the exposure of the Holy of Holies at the time of the earthquake which followed Jesus' death, would have profoundly disturbed them and reawakened their anxieties.[6]

Secondly, the Gospel of Peter may shed some light on the course of events. This apocryphal gospel has some mythological features and is at some points in conflict with Matthew (e.g. in placing the sealing of the tomb on the Friday evening), but it is fairly early in date and many scholars believe that some of its independent features may represent genuine historical recollections.[7] This gospel says that there was great disquiet among the people at the crucifixion of Jesus and at the 'great signs' which accompanied it and that this murmuring of the people made the elders afraid. It goes on to say further that a crowd gathered at the sepulchre on Saturday morning. If the authorities sensed a growing public sympathy for Jesus and a growing condemnation of their actions, the prospect of what might happen when the restraint of the sabbath observance was removed would alarm them.

Thirdly, there were dark mutterings about a supposed prediction of resurrection by Jesus which worried them. There is certainly no reason why the Jewish authorities should not have heard talk about a resurrection on the third day. It is true that Jesus' predictions were made mainly to his followers and not to the public, though on at least one occasion in the Galilean ministry he spoke openly to some Pharisees.[8] It is true also that, although his disciples did not grasp what he meant at the time, his words were perfectly clear and known to a good many people, including of course Judas Iscariot. In the desperate attempt to find evidence to incriminate Jesus, the chief priests had eventually picked on his alleged statement: "I will destroy this temple that is made with hands, and in three days I will build another, not made with hands."[9] In their search for watertight evidence they must have weighed every word, and it is hardly likely that Jesus' sayings about his rising on the third day would not have come to their ears. So it is probable that they really did fear the consequences of a successful plot to simulate a resurrection.

They feared trouble for which they would be held responsible. The body of Jesus, which should have been a Roman responsibility, had become a Jewish responsibility by the wholly unforeseen and disconcerting act of Joseph in asking for its custody. The chief priests were most anxious that it should again become a Roman responsibility. So, despite the rebuff over the wording of the superscription on the cross,[10] they risked a further interview with the disgruntled governor to obtain a detachment of soldiers to serve as guard.

It is not wholly clear in what terms Pilate responded to their request as his reply is ambiguous in the Greek. It could be either: "You have a guard" or "Have a guard". If it was the former, it would be a blank refusal, compelling them to fall back on their own temple guard, whose members were already utterly weary with their exhausting Passover duties, which had unexpectedly included the unusual task on the previous Thursday night. In this case, it would not be at all surprising that next day they could tell their tale, which might well have been true, that they had fallen asleep; nor that they should have reported their strange experiences to the high priests, nor that they were bribed to tell a lie.

On the whole, however, it seems better to take his reply as an accession to their request: "Yes, take a military guard and make the tomb as secure as possible." And this for two reasons. Firstly, while Pilate might easily have used his own Latin word 'custodia' to describe the temple guard, it is not likely that Matthew would have called its members 'soldiers'. As Edersheim says, they "were neither regularly armed nor trained. Nor would the Romans have tolerated a regular armed Jewish force in Jerusalem."[11]

Secondly, it seems that the services of the Roman cohort stationed in the Antonia Castle had been called upon for the arrest in Gethsemane. While at first glance it might appear from the synoptists that Judas had been accompanied only by a motley crowd of ill-armed servants of the hierarchy, closer examination shows that it was 'a great crowd', which included some of the chief priests and elders in person and captains of the temple guard, and also (according to John) a chiliarch and cohort.[12] The fact that the arrest of Jesus was not just a domestic affair directed by the Sanhedrin, but was authorised by Pilate, is strikingly confirmed by Pilate's wife's dream. Before going to sleep on Thursday night she had evidently heard about it and knew what was likely to happen. So next morning (Matthew tells us) "while he was sitting on the judgment seat, his wife sent word to him, 'Have nothing to do with that righteous man, for I have suffered much over him today in a dream' "[13]

It is a great mistake to underestimate the anxiety which the following of Jesus caused the authorities. On the one hand was its sheer size. There was clearly massive support for Jesus before the passion; and even after the fiery ordeal of the crucifixion, we read of an appearance to 500 brothers at once and (in Jerusalem itself) of 3,000 converts in a single day. On the other hand was its Galilean complexion. Galilee was a hotbed of Messianic expectations and of zealot unrest. The authorities were aware of the seething discontent which was eventually to issue in the fearful war of AD 66–70. There had been a number of disquieting occurrences: the insurrection of Barabbas had been recently quelled; Pilate had been involved in an ugly incident, in which he had mingled the blood of Galileans with their sacrifices;[14] only a few days previously Jesus had made a royal entry into the capital. All this meant that Pilate would be inclined to listen seriously to suggestions by the chief priests on matters of security. Thus it seems right to believe that a distinguished deputation had waited on the governor in order to procure a strong reserve of soldiers for the arrest. Apparently Judas and the temple guard had gone on ahead, while the chief priests and soldiers had followed behind. Only when it came to the binding of Jesus had the chiliarch stepped into the limelight.

The Gospel of Peter seems to suggest that the policy adopted at Gethsemane was followed also in Joseph's garden. Not only did Pilate send a Roman guard, but "with them there came elders and scribes to the sepulchre" and the elders were also keeping watch. In other words, the Romans took seriously the need to contain the Galilean danger, but they preferred to back up the Jews, rather than to relieve them of their responsibilities. If that was the case detachments of soldiers and of temple guards went to Joseph's garden. The stone was securely sealed and a watch set up of men tired out with the extra duties of recent days and particularly with the long duties of Thursday night.

So as Saturday drew to its close, there were (on our best reckoning) *at Bethany* nine apostles, now joined by the two Marys and Clopas. These three doubtless slept uneasily listening for cock crow, anxious to set out for the city at the first streaks of daylight. *In John's house* were Peter and John and Jesus' mother, Zebedee and Salome, the last named expecting the arrival of the two Marys shortly after dawn. *In the Hasmonean palace* were Joanna and 'Susanna'. They were not involved in the domestic affairs of Salome and the Marys and it seems likely that they acted independently of them from the time of their consultation after the burial till they met again at the tomb for the anointing. They were intending to make their own way to the tomb when there was light enough for them to work by in its dark interior. *In Joseph's peaceful garden* were two groups of guards beginning their vigil.

CHAPTER 7

Early on Easter Sunday Morning

THE EARTHQUAKE

The first event of Easter Sunday morning is contained in Matthew's vivid account:

> Now after the sabbath, toward the dawn of the first day of the week, Mary Magdalene and the other Mary went to see the sepulchre.
>
> And behold, there was a great earthquake; for an angel of the Lord descended from heaven and came and rolled back the stone, and sat upon it. His appearance was like lightning, and his raiment white as snow. And for fear of him the guards trembled and became like dead men.
>
> But the angel said to the women, 'Do not be afraid; for I know that you seek Jesus who was crucified. He is not here; for he has risen, as he said. Come, see the place where he lay. Then go quickly and tell his disciples that he has risen from the dead, and behold, he is going before you to Galilee; there you will see him. Lo, I have told you.' So they departed quickly from the tomb with fear and great joy, and ran to tell his disciples. And behold, Jesus met them and said, 'Hail!' And they came up and took hold of his feet and worshipped him. Then Jesus said to them, 'Do not be afraid; go and tell my brethren to go to Galilee, and there they will see me.'
>
> While they were going, behold, some of the guard went into the city and told the chief priests all that had taken place. And when they had assembled with the elders and taken counsel, they gave a sum of money to the soldiers and said, 'Tell people, "His disciples

came by night and stole him away while we were asleep." And if this comes to the governor's ears, we will satisfy him and keep you out of trouble.' So they took the money and did as they were directed; and this story has been spread among the Jews to this day.

(Matthew 28:1–15)

On a superficial reading it would seem that the great earthquake took place after the women had arrived and that the guards lay prostrate on the ground while the angel delivered his message. But on deeper reflection it becomes clear that it is unlikely that Matthew intended his readers to understand this. Such a notion is contrary to the thrust of the rest of the New Testament. Peter is quoted in Acts 10:41 as saying that God did not make Jesus manifest "to all the people but to us who were chosen by God as witnesses". He was seen by selected witnesses only, not by the people of Israel generally, still less by heathen soldiers. It hardly seems likely that pagans were allowed to hear the first utterance of "He is risen". It is possible that Matthew might have thought that they heard a sound but not the words, as had been the case in an incident which had occurred a few days before,[1] but if so he gives no hint of it.

The suggested picture is an incongruous one: the guards lying about like dead men while the women approach the dazzling angel, while the angel delivers his message outside the tomb, while he brings the women into the tomb and instructs them there and while the women rush out of the garden. It is better to suppose that (without spelling out the details) he intends his readers to understand that the soldiers left shortly before the women arrived and that their seeking of an interview with some of the chief priests coincided with the women's reporting to the disciples. In other words, Matthew intends us to understand that the angel rolled back the stone, not to let the body out, but to let the witnesses in, in proof of the resurrection. He sat in awesome splendour on the great gravestone, making it clear that no one could replace it. He sat there to frighten the guard away, and then presumably went inside not to frighten the women unnecessarily. He told them that *they* were not to be afraid.[2]

If this was really Matthew's intention, it may be asked why he wrote so ambiguously. We have to remember that first century writers had to work without the help of such modern aids as parenthesising brackets, and that, since Greeks care little about relative time, the use of the pluperfect tense was much less favoured by them than by us. Often in the New Testament the aorist tense needs to be rendered by an English pluperfect.[3] So Matthew 28:2–4 could be inserted in brackets and translated with no impropriety:

> (And behold there had been a great earthquake. For an angel of the Lord had descended from heaven, and had come and rolled back the stone, and sat upon it. His appearance was like lightning, and his raiment white as snow. And for fear of him the guards had trembled and become like dead men.)

Such a translation, however, exaggerates the element of relative time in a manner alien to the Greek (or, for that matter, Semitic) mind. W.E. Brown, commenting on Matthew's usage, here makes some interesting remarks about the methods of ancient historiography:

> The great historians of the nineteenth century learned to solve their problems by keeping to a chronological order. Such a practice is strictly speaking impossible unless the narration is confined to one person or to one locality .... Earlier chroniclers had tackled the difficulty in two ways. Sometimes they incorporated in a single story a number of actions and speeches which had a common theme, not indicating at all the time of the occurrence. Sometimes they jumped back and forward between two or more parallel sequences of events, leaving it to the reader to understand that each item is as it were a flash on a cinema screen.[4]

We may thus conclude that the earthquake took place before the arrival of any women and that the terrified guards had already left by the time they arrived. It was presumably a recurrence of the earth tremors which had caused the rending of the massive curtain which divided the Holy Place from the Holy of Holies at the time of the crucifixion. That the geological structure is conducive to violent shocks at this point has been brought home vividly to the many visitors who have seen the Church of the Holy Sepulchre shored up because of seismic damage.

THE STORY OF THE STOLEN BODY

The story of the setting of the guard is one of the most extraordinary pieces of Christian apologetic ever written. As we have said, it bristles with improbabilities at every point: the sabbath visit to the governor, the great earthquake, the flashing angel rolling back the stone, the reporting to the chief priests, the bribe to the soldiers to tell the tale *that they were asleep on duty* — everything invites, not belief, but incredulity. And how stupid, having introduced the useful apologetic idea of a closely guarded tomb, to give a handle to the opposition by even hinting that the guards did not do their job! It is a worthless piece of Christian apologetic at whatever date it was written, *unless it happens to be undeniably true.* It would have been at its most effective if published in Jerusalem at a time when the church was under bitter attack, as for instance when the church was scattered through Saul's persecution, or at the time of the murder of the apostle James in AD 42. Periods of persecution must have been dangerous for those who had the courage to stay in Jerusalem, and anything to provoke curiosity about their doings would have been unwelcome. Is this perhaps why Matthew mentions only the actions of Joseph of Arimathea, which were well known to the authorities and which were essential to his apologetic, and then switches all attention to far away Galilee? It is possible also that Matthew's colourless description of the women going to 'see' the tomb is designed not to provoke the thought that the followers of Jesus did, on their own confession, plan to interfere with the body. In any case the publication of the true facts, which would be privately, if not publicly, confirmed by a large number of people who had either experienced them or had heard the original report, would have been a valuable defence of the Christian faith. The story of the behaviour of the guard may have reached the Christians through the two believing members of the Sanhedrin or possibly this vivid account may have come directly from one of those present.[5]

Matthew tells us that the story of the stolen body "has been spread among the Jews to this day," in other words it was current at the time of writing. 'To this day' would have been appropriate two years after the event or two hundred. There is an artlessness about the official story — for if the soldiers had been asleep, how could they have told who stole the body?[6] Yet this was undoubtedly the story that was put around. It is given as the current report when the gospel was written, and it is independently attested by Justin Martyr. Justin was born in Palestine about AD 100 of pagan parents. He became a Christian in about

AD 130 and for a time taught in Ephesus. He wrote there (c. AD 155) his *Disputation with Trypho the Jew*, in which he said, without fear of contradiction by his sharp-witted antagonist, "You have sent chosen and ordained men throughout all the world to proclaim that ... his disciples stole him by night from the tomb."[7] As giving the Jewish version of the events it is a back-handed testimony to the fact of the empty tomb. When it is asked if it is likely that the solders would accept a bribe to plead guilty to sleeping on duty (an offence punishable by death), it is overlooked that an equally serious breach of discipline had already been committed in the flight from the tomb. Soldiers and priests and Pilate evidently believed that something supernatural had happened, hence the willingness of the authorities to screen the soldiers.

This fits well with the statement of Matthew that "some of the guard" went to the chief priests. It is natural to suppose that it was Jewish guards who encouraged the senior Roman soldiers to go first with them to their authorities, rather than to report their mortal misdemeanours direct to Pilate. They doubtless judged rightly that Caiaphas might be a useful buffer between them and the governor. The chief priests on their part must have greeted the report with anger and consternation. They would have had no scruples about pinning the blame on the guard and securing their punishment, if it had been practicable; but it would have done nothing to prevent the circulation of their dangerous and damaging story. The only hope of the chief priests was to seek the cooperation of the guards in spreading another story of their own invention.

It would seem that the great earthquake was not long before the arrival of the women, though it is difficult to say how long. Matthew says that the guard reported to the chief priests, a council was assembled and decisions taken — all of which would have occupied a considerable time. If the initial reporting to the chief priests was literally while the women were on their way to tell the brethren, the incident in the garden must have been quite a short time before the women's arrival, but it is doubtful whether Matthew should be taken so literally. There may have been a considerable interval. At any rate, when the guards had gone, the angel who had sat outside to frighten the men away, withdrew into the tomb so as not to frighten the women away.

THE ARRIVAL OF THE WOMEN

At what time did the women arrive? The four reports run as follows:

Matthew	Mark	Luke	John
Now after the sabbath, toward the dawn of the first day of the week, MM and the other Mary went to see the sepulchre. (28:1)	Very early on the first day of the week they went to the tomb when the sun had risen. (16:2)	On the first day of the week, at early dawn they went to the tomb. (24:1)	On the first day of the week MM came to the tomb early, while it was still dark. (20:1)

There is a fairly close agreement of testimony here ("toward the dawn", "very early", "at early dawn", "while it was still dark") except for Mark, who has the appearance of contradicting himself. In the ancient world "very early" would hardly describe what we mean by "when the sun had risen". In our day (to use the language of the Nautical Almanac) "sunrise denotes the moment when the upper limb of the sun appears to be on the horizon" — which is broad daylight. Sunrise in biblical usage, however, means break of day. We have an Old Testament account of a dawn attack taking place "as soon as the sun is up", and a psalm which refers to the night animals returning to their lairs "when the sun rises".[8] So Mark is not contradicting himself, he is referring to a time when day had broken.

There is perhaps no need to insist upon any distinction between Matthew's "toward the dawn", Mark's "very early", Luke's "early dawn" and John's "while it was still dark". Darkness and light are relative terms and it would be perfectly possible, and not inaccurate, for one person to describe the time as "early dawn" which another described as "still dark". It needs to be remembered, however, that it could have been undeniably dark on the women's departure and undeniably light on their arrival, particularly if their starting-point were Bethany. Furthermore, it should be noted that the words "went" in Matthew, Mark and Luke translate the same verb as the "came" in John and that either translation would be possible in any of the cases, it depending on what standpoint the writer is thought to be

adopting. If John is thinking of Mary Magdalene setting off from
Bethany, the translation "went to the tomb early, while it was
still dark" would be precisely accurate. Similarly Matthew's
"toward the dawn ... went" suggests the same Bethany standpoint — the two Marys started their journey just before dawn.
Mark's "very early" could well represent Peter's recollection of
the Marys and Salome leaving John's house and Luke's "at early
dawn" would fit well enough the departure of Joanna and
'Susanna' from the Hasmonean palace. These distinctions may
be too fine, but we undoubtedly get a consistent and coherent
picture if we see the first departures as being in the dark and the
last arrivals as being before sunrise.

What was the order of events? If our earlier reasoned conjectures are correct, we must picture something like this. Mary
Magdalene, the other Mary and Clopas had set off from Bethany
while it was still dark. By the time they had arrived at John's
house it was getting quite light. Anointing was women's work, so
Clopas went no further, but the two Marys, joined now by
Salome with the ointments, continued on their way. They went

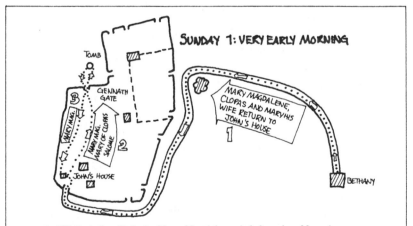

1. While it is still dark, Mary Magdalene and the other Mary (accompanied by her husband Clopas) set off from Bethany to return to
   John's house.
   (There is an earthquake, the angel removes the grave-stone and the
   guard flees.)
2. Clopas stays at Johns house, while Salome joins the two Marys and
   the three proceed to the garden via the Gennath Gate.
3. They see the grave open. Mary Magdalene runs back to tell John
   and Peter.

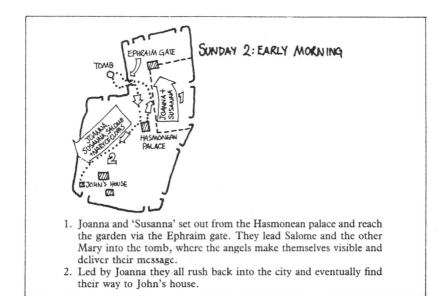

SUNDAY 2: EARLY MORNING

1. Joanna and 'Susanna' set out from the Hasmonean palace and reach the garden via the Ephraim gate. They lead Salome and the other Mary into the tomb, where the angels make themselves visible and deliver their message.
2. Led by Joanna they all rush back into the city and eventually find their way to John's house.

out through the Gennath gate to Joseph's garden. There is nothing to suggest that they were troubled by the "great" earthquake. ("Great" of course is also a relative term, but a tremor in pitch darkness, accompanied by the sudden arrival of an angel in brilliant white whose "appearance was like lightning", might well be deemed "great", even if its effects were light and localised.) They were troubled by another matter — how to move the big gravestone. They were probably reassured by the recollection that Joseph had a gardener (or more probably a night watchman)[9] who could well still be on duty. By the time they reached the garden it was full daylight and as they approached the tomb they saw to their astonishment that the great stone had been rolled right away from the entrance.

Mary Magdalene at once jumped to the conclusion that the body had been taken. She dashed off to tell Peter and John, leaving the two older women standing there lost for words. After a few moments they began to discuss what to do, but before they had decided on a line of action they saw Joanna and 'Susanna' approaching, having come as agreed to join them in completing the burial rites. They had come from the Hasmonean palace via the Ephraim gate. The newcomers, who had already been inside the tomb on Friday evening, had no indecision. They insisted that at least they should look to see whether the body had in fact gone. Joanna led the way. They stooped down and passed through the entrance into the open space that lay beyond. They stood against the wall on their left as they entered to get accustomed to the dim light.

INSIDE THE TOMB

The three synoptists tell the story of what follows:

Matthew	Mark	Luke
The angel said to the women, 'Do not be afraid; for I know that you seek Jesus who was crucified. He is not here; for he has risen, as he said. Come, see the place where he lay. Then go quickly and tell his disciples that he has risen from the dead, and behold, he is going before you to Galilee; there you will see him. Lo, I have told you.' *(28:5–7)*	Entering the tomb, they saw a young man sitting on the right side, dressed in a white robe; and they were amazed. And he said to them, 'Do not be amazed; you seek Jesus of Nazareth, who was crucified. He has risen, he is not here; see the place where they laid him. But go, tell his disciples and Peter that he is going before you to Galilee; there you will see him, as he told you.' *(16:5–7)*	When they went in they did not find the body. While they were perplexed about this, behold, two men stood by them in dazzling apparel; and as they were frightened and bowed their faces to the ground, the men said to them, 'Why do you seek the living among the dead? Remember how he told you, while he was still in Galilee, that the Son of man must be delivered into the hands of sinful men, and be crucified, and on the third day rise.' And they remembered his words. *(24:3–8)*

When these stories are compared it is clear that Luke's account is strikingly different from those of Matthew and Mark, especially in the record of the angels' message.[10] There is no 'Fear not', no invitation to see where he was laid, no command to tell the disciples, no promise of seeing him in Galilee. Instead the messengers say, "Why do you seek the living among the dead?" And in place of Mark's "There you will see him, as he told you," they say "Remember how he told you, while he was still in Galilee, that the Son of man must be delivered into the hands of sinful men, and be crucified, and on the third day rise." The different reference to Galilee is particularly noteworthy. Whereas Matthew and Mark look forward to Jesus about to go ahead of them to Galilee, Luke looks back and refers to what Jesus told them when they were together in Galilee. Although there are enough links to show that Luke is describing the same happening as the other two, there is nothing to suggest that the wording has a common source, oral or literary. We may well believe that Luke is relating Joanna's story.

With regard to Matthew and Mark, however, the resemblances are much closer. They are not so close as to suggest that one is copying the other, but rather that they derive from a time when the apostles heard the story in similar words. Matthew's account could be very close to the way he first heard it and Mark's to the way Peter first heard it — which included the unforgettable: "Go tell his disciples and Peter." There is nothing in any of the three messages which is contradictory to anything in either of the others, the matter is complementary. All that is recorded could have been uttered without hurry in a couple of minutes.

A DIGRESSION ON ANGELS

Before we consider the message and its aftermath, it is necessary to look at the messengers. Mark speaks of "a young man sitting on the right side, dressed in a white robe" and says "they were amazed" and eventually they "fled from the tomb; for trembling and astonishment had come upon them .. for they were afraid." Although the figure is described simply as a "young man", the whole scene is depicted as one of awe and fear, partly evoked by the nature of his white robe. He was a supernatural young man. In other words he was an angel, depicted as all biblical angels are, not as a winged creature, but as a man.[11] In Luke's story it is even more clear that his two men are angels: "While they were perplexed about this, behold, two men stood by them in dazzling apparel; ... they were frightened and bowed their faces to the ground."

The translation "stood by", which would bring Luke into contradiction with Mark's "sitting", cannot be insisted on. The word is frequently used meaning "to appear to", often implying suddenness.[12] When the angels appeared in the little cave room, they may well have appeared in a sitting position, very much as Mary Magdalene saw them on her later visit — a position calculated to minimise the alarm that their sudden presence was bound to cause. Matthew and Mark do not make it clear that the angels appeared after the women had entered, but both stress the awesomeness of the figures they encountered. One might have inferred even from their accounts that had the women seen such dazzling figures from the doorway they would have been too frightened to have ventured in. But only Luke says explicitly that the women had gone into the tomb before the appearance of the angels. The mention of *two* men is one of the many differences between Mark and Luke which makes them look like two independent narratives. Of Matthew's angel it was also said that "his appearance was like lightning and his raiment white as snow." We have argued that he had withdrawn into the cave before the women arrived, so that his "Come, see the place where he lay"[13] is not an invitation to enter the tomb, but to put away their fears and take a close look at the grave space (now empty save for burial linen).

Legend or History?

There is much scepticism about angels who conveniently appear and disappear as required. This is reasonable enough for those who deny the supernatural altogether, but for those who accept the substantial truth of the accounts of the appearances of Jesus, it is quite unreasonable, and it impoverishes our view of that part of the creation which is usually hidden from our sight. The biblical belief in God-sent 'messengers' who appear briefly and then disappear again is based mainly on the testimony of trusted witnesses, including Jesus himself. (Jesus is quoted as speaking of angels at least twenty times). In the case of the Easter angels the testimony comes from the very women who reported the appearance of Jesus. If their testimony is true, angels look like men; they move; they speak; and they disappear at will. It is all of a piece with the manifestations of Jesus himself after the resurrection.

One or Two?

It should be said once and for all that the mention by one evangelist of two angels and by another of one does not constitute a contradiction or discrepancy. If there were two, there was one. When learned critics make heavy weather about the accuracy of such accounts, they lack common sense. Contradiction would only be created if the writer who mentioned the one should go on to say explicitly that there was only one. In a scene where one person is the chief speaker or actor it would often be perfectly natural to omit reference to the irrelevant fact that he had a companion. Indeed this provides the best explanation of the various incidents in which one evangelist mentions two people and another only one (e.g. Matthew's two demoniacs at Gadara (8:28) and two blind men at Jericho (20:30)). In the repeated telling of the incident about the two, it could become increasingly clear that only one had a function in the story and that the other was superfluous. It would be natural to drop the latter and thereby leave a simpler, less cluttered narrative. The notion that Matthew (or, in the case of the angels, Luke) doubled the numbers to heighten the miraculous is to impugn both the veracity and common sense of the writer. It needs to be remembered that we are dealing with two *descriptions* of an event, and not with two witnesses replying to cross-examination. If witnesses, who had been in the tomb at the same time, had been asked independently, "Precisely how many men did you see?" and had given different answers, that would have shown one or other to be unreliable. But these witnesses are not answering the question "How many?", they are giving (as all descriptions must be) incomplete descriptions of a complex event.

The Succession of Events

Piecing together the data to obtain the whole story, it would seem that there were two angels, one more prominent than the other. They (or he) first lifted the great stone and rolled it from the entrance and then sat upon it till the guards had left. They then retired inside and were invisible when the first women arrived. They made themselves visible to them and delivered their message. When Peter and John arrived they were again invisible, but they had reappeared when Mary Magdalene looked into the tomb.

THE MESSAGE AND THE FLIGHT FROM THE TOMB

So we must imagine the four women against the wall in the cave. Suddenly, the darkness is lit up. They see two men in dazzling white, sitting by the grave-space where the body of Jesus had lain. The women bow their faces to the ground in utter consternation. Then one of the angels speaks. (Putting together the accounts of the synoptists) he says:

> Don't you be afraid. I know whom you are seeking — Jesus the Nazarene, the crucified one. Why do you seek the living among the dead? He is not here — for he is risen, as he said. Come, see the place where they laid him. Remember how he talked to you when he was in Galilee, saying that the Son of man must be betrayed into the hands of sinful men and be crucified and on the third day rise. Go quickly, tell his disciples (and Peter) that he is raised from the dead and is going before you into Galilee. You will see him there, as he said.

The women's response is given by the synoptists.

Matthew	Mark	Luke
So they departed quickly from the tomb with fear and great joy, and ran to tell his disciples. *(28:8)*	They went out and fled from the tomb; for trembling and astonishment had come upon them; and they said nothing to any one, for they were afraid. *(16:8)*	Returning from the tomb they told all this to the eleven and to all the rest. Now it was Mary Magdalene and Joanna and Mary the mother of James and the other women with them who told this to the apostles; but these words seemed to them an idle tale, and they did not believe them. *(24:9–11)*

Mark's version, being supposedly the earliest and most authentic account and being (according to scholarly consensus) the conclusion to his gospel, has received the greatest attention. It is commonly said that the gospel ends with the women keeping absolute silence. But this is surely absurd. Presumably they said nothing to any one else, perhaps not even to one another, on the way to tell Peter and John. But clearly the whole story came streaming out eventually. How else could anyone have known it? The meaning of "trembling and astonishment" may not be so very far from Matthew's "fear and great joy". Paul in an epistle much concerned with Christian joy uses the expression "fear and trembling" to describe the devout Christian's attitude to the presence of God.[14] The "astonishment" or "ecstasy" may include the idea that the women, though dazed and trembling, were borne along on the wings of an awesome joy.

Luke's account evidently telescopes the coming of Mary Magdalene to Peter and John (giving her pride of place in the list of women) and the coming of Joanna and other women to the eleven *and to the rest*. (He shows himself conscious that others beside the eleven were informed.) He also strikes the unbelief motif which the next eight verses of Mark is going to emphasise. So we may picture Joanna leading 'Susanna', Salome and the other Mary back into the city by the way she had come, through the Ephraim gate. At first utterly speechless, scarcely knowing where they were going, their fear and bewilderment mingled with a great joy, they soon found themselves at John's house bursting to tell the astonishing news. The happenings in the garden since the women first arrived had probably taken less than ten minutes.

CHAPTER 8

The First Appearances

The next event is recorded by John:

> Now on the first day of the week Mary Magdalene came to the tomb early, while it was still dark, and saw that the stone had been taken away from the tomb. So she ran, and went to Simon Peter and the other disciple, the one whom Jesus loved, and said to them, "They have taken the Lord out of the tomb, and we do not know where they have laid him." Peter then came out with the other disciple, and they went toward the tomb. They both ran, but the other disciple outran Peter and reached the tomb first; and stooping to look in, he saw the linen cloths lying there, but he did not go in. Then Simon Peter came, following him, and went into the tomb; he saw the linen cloths lying, and the napkin, which had been on his head, not lying with the linen cloths but rolled up in a place by itself. Then the other disciple, who reached the tomb first, also went in, and he saw and believed; for as yet they did not know the scripture, that he must rise from the dead. Then the disciples went back to their homes.
>
> *(John 20:1-10)*

John mentions only Mary Magdalene as visiting the tomb. If it is true that John is supplementing the other gospels, he would of course have been aware that other women were there, but would be deliberately confining himself to the one story which he wishes to tell, and which doubtless had made a tremendous impact upon him when he first heard it from Mary's own breathless lips. There are some confirmatory indications that this is so. Mary's words 'we do not know where they have laid him' clearly imply the presence of other women. John also represents Mary as going 'while it was still dark', which a woman would scarcely have ventured to do unaccompanied.

Latham[1] supposed that the other women had gone to the tomb independently and had looked into the tomb before Mary's arrival, and had reported its emptiness to her when she arrived shortly after. This seems improbable as Mary is always mentioned first. Furthermore, the thought of resurrection (which the angel's message would have given her) does not appear to have been in her mind, only the thought that no one would have removed the stone unless it was to take away the body. John's account strongly suggests that she came and went before anyone had entered the tomb. Perhaps the earth-tremors had made her jumpy, so that one look at the open tomb was enough to make her run to the apostles.

As soon as Peter and John heard her news, they set out for the tomb running. Clopas as an older man was doubtless content to stay behind with Jesus' mother. Because of the many alternative routes through the ancient city those on the way from the tomb did not meet those who were going to the tomb. John, who was a local resident, knew the most direct way from his house, through the Gennath gate. But Joanna, who was only an occasional visitor to the city, was (we may conjecture) less sure in her sense of direction, only knowing the position of John's house in its relation to the Hasmonean palace. It seems probable, as we have suggested, that she led her party back by the way she had come, via the Ephraim gate.

John's full story is in line with a short, but disputed, account in Luke 24:12: "Peter rose and ran to the tomb; stooping and looking in, he saw the linen cloths by themselves; and he went home wondering at what had happened." When Luke says that Peter saw the linen cloths "by themselves" he presumably means simply that he saw *only* linen cloths – no body. Although this verse is not found in some manuscripts the RSV is not justified in omitting it. Some have argued that it was a later addition borrowed from the Gospel of John. But in this account of the visit to the tomb there is no reference to any other disciple, which shows independence of the later gospel, rather than a borrowing from it. It is better to suppose that when John came to write he supplemented Luke's account and added his own attestation. It should be noted, however, that although Luke only mentions Peter, he shows himself aware of the presence of more than one person when he quotes the Emmaus disciples as saying that in addition to the women 'some of those who were with us went to the tomb' (24:24). John fills in the story with vivid details, most of which seem to have no theological significance, but are simply recounted the way they were remembered. That John reached the tomb first could have been because he was the younger man. (Peter was leader of the twelve and may well therefore have been older than John, but even so youth and fleetness of foot are not synonymous.) John, more diffident than Peter, peers into the tomb and sees the grave-cloths. The impulsive Peter goes in, and John follows.

Having entered John 'saw and believed'. He may here be countering the impression which might have been gained from Mark and Luke that the unbelief of the men was total. He dates the beginning of the revival of his own faith from the moment he saw the disposition of grave-cloths (*othonia*) and napkin (*soudarion*). What precisely it was that convinced him is not clear. It may be that it was the mere sight of burial-wrappings and no body which persuaded him — he realised that neither friend nor foe would have carefully removed the coverings and then carried a naked corpse through the Jerusalem suburbs. Or had he something more in mind? John gives prominence to the fact that he saw 'the napkin, which had been on his head, not lying with the linen cloths but rolled up in a place by itself.' Some have supposed that he was describing burial-wrappings that had collapsed after the body had passed through them. But in that case the head-covering and the body-covering would have been almost, if not quite, touching each other; also we should not have expected the napkin to have been described as 'rolled up'. It will be noted that John nowhere mentions the linen sheet or shroud (*sindon*) which the other three evangelists describe. If a sheet had covered the whole body, the napkin would not have been visible after the body had passed through it, but would have remained hidden beneath it. Of interest is the mention by Luke in 23:53 of a linen shroud or sheet (*sindon* – in the singular) and here of *the linen cloths* (*othonia* – in the plural). The former is the word used by Matthew and Mark and the latter by John.

It has to be acknowledged that from the gospel texts alone it is not possible to say precisely what these terms mean, since both *sindon* and *othonia* have a wide range of closely similar uses. *Sindon* would certainly be a suitable word for a large sheet or shroud, and it is commonly so translated, but in itself it means no more than a piece of linen. *Othonia* is either a diminutive word which would be suitable to describe small pieces of linen, or it could be an adjective of quality used as a noun, in which case it could refer to linen pieces of any size, including a large sheet. In other words, the *othonia* might be the bandages which bound wrists and ankles or they might include the shroud as well. One thing seems clear: John is not describing burial-cloths which collapsed in situ with the removal of the body, he is showing that the *soudarion* at least had been folded up by supernatural hands and moved to a separate place.[2] He saw, not disorder left by grave robbers, but the visible tokens of his master set free from the bonds of death.

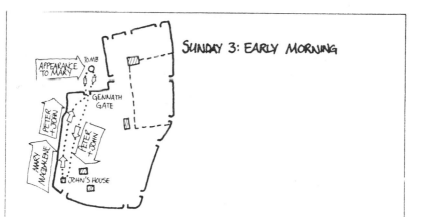

1. Meanwhile John and Peter (followed shortly by Mary Magdalene) have set off for the tomb by the Gennath Gate, and they see the empty tomb.
2. As they return home, Mary Magdalene lingers behind. She sees the angels in the tomb and then Jesus appears to her.
3. She returns to John's house.

After this (according to the RSV), 'the disciples went back to their homes.' This translation implies that they came from more than one home, but the Greek could equally well be translated 'home', which tallies better with John's account, which suggests that they started out from the same house.[3]

THE APPEARANCE TO MARY MAGDALENE

In the meantime Mary Magdalene, who must have spent a little while talking to the Lord's mother, returned to the garden. There she found herself entirely alone. John recounts the story that she told him:

> But Mary stood weeping outside the tomb, and as she wept she stooped to look into the tomb; and she saw two angels in white, sitting where the body of Jesus had lain, one at the head and one at the feet. They said to her, "Woman, why are you weeping?" She said to them, "Because they have taken away my Lord, and I do not know where they have laid him." Saying this, she turned round and saw Jesus standing, but she did not know that it was Jesus. Jesus said to her, "Woman, why are you weeping? Whom do you seek?" Supposing him to be the gardener, she said to him, "Sir, if you have carried him away, tell me where you have laid him, and I will take him away." Jesus said to her, "Mary." She turned and said to him in Hebrew, "Rabboni!" (which means Teacher). Jesus said to her, "Do not hold me, for I have not yet ascended to the Father; but go to my brethren and say to them, I am ascending to my Father and your Father, to my God and your God." Mary Magdalene went and said to the disciples, "I have seen the Lord"; and she told them that he had said these things to her.
>
> *(John 20:11–18)*

There are several indications that the appearances of angels to Mary Magdalene and to the other women were quite distinct. The appearance to Mary was after she had reported to the apostles, to the others before. Mary apparently saw the angels (though not in terrifying brightness) from the entrance, the others were startled by their sudden appearance after they had come inside. The discourse in the two cases is also quite different; Mary is asked why she is weeping, she gives her reply, and then sees Jesus; the other women are spoken to at some length, they make no reply, and they leave the garden without seeing Jesus. The distinctness is shown at this particulr point in the story by the subtle change from the first person plural to the first person singular. When Mary told her story to the apostles she had just left the other women and could say '*We* do not know where they have laid him,' but now she is quite on her own and says '*I* do not know where they have laid him.'

Similarly the appearance of Jesus to Mary seems quite distinct from his appearance to the other women recorded by Matthew (see below). The first is individual, the second is collective; in the first Jesus comes up quietly from behind, in the second Jesus meets them and hails them; the discourse in the two cases is also quite different. Furthermore, superficially at least there is a striking difference in the way Mary is told not to hold Jesus, whereas the other women do so without rebuke. John's use of the present tense here, however, might be paraphrased, 'Do not cling to me.'[4] He is not forbidding her to touch him, but giving her a gentle reassurance that she need not fear to leave him and tell her good news to others, for his ascension to the Father is not just yet. An undesigned coincidence of a very indirect kind may perhaps be seen in Mary's 'supposing him to be the gardener'. Why should she so immediately think particularly of the gardener? Mark seems to provide the answer: they had already discussed the problem of removing the great stone and had probably thought of the 'gardener' (or night watchman) as the most likely helper.

THE APPEARANCE TO THE OTHER WOMEN

As the two appearances are distinct, that to Mary Magdalene must be put first (as Mark 16:9 says) and the second must be put at a sufficient interval after the women's flight from the tomb to allow for all the comings and goings recorded by John. So then Mary returned to John's house to find a group of excited women and a group of confused and somewhat sceptical men. The women's commission was less than half fulfilled with nine disciples in Bethany still uninformed, so presumably two or more of them agreed forthwith to tell them the news. The likeliest volunteers would seem to be Salome, mother of James the elder, and Mary, mother of James the younger. Matthew tells their story in the briefest terms:

> They ... ran to tell his disciples. And behold, Jesus met them and said, "Hail!" And they came up and took hold of his feet and worshipped him. Then Jesus said to them, "Do not be afraid; go and tell my brethren to go to Galilee, and there they will see me."
>
> (*Matthew 28:8–10*)

If it was in fact Salome and the other Mary who went on this errand, it would mean that the other Mary had different companions on the journey into Jerusalem in early morning and on this journey back to Bethany a little later. Mary Magdalene went in with her, and Salome joined her coming out. As this is irrelevant to Matthew's concerns it is not surprising that he does not mention it. Mary Magdalene after all did report her seeing of the Lord to some disciples, even if she did not go to Bethany to tell the nine.

One must picture this meeting somewhere on the track between Jerusalem and Bethany, that is to say, on some part of the Mount of Olives. The women saw him, came up to him, fell on their knees and held his feet. Jesus told them not to fear, but

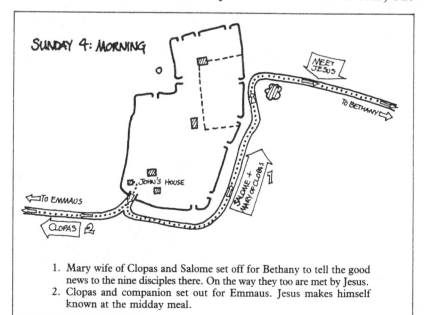

1. Mary wife of Clopas and Salome set off for Bethany to tell the good news to the nine disciples there. On the way they too are met by Jesus.
2. Clopas and companion set out for Emmaus. Jesus makes himself known at the midday meal.

to go and deliver a message to his 'brethren'. The emphasis here is more on proclamation and promise than on direct command. The sentence might be translated: 'Announce to my brothers that they are to go to Galilee and they will see me there.' It is a message for the brethren generally and not only for the eleven. It should be observed that the message of the angel had been 'Go quickly and tell his *disciples*' — 'disciples' being a broader term than 'apostles', representing hundreds of followers, not just eleven. It was natural that the apostles should be among the first to be told, but it was in fact a proclamation to all Christ's brethren that they were to return to Galilee to see him there. Matthew records the journey of the eleven to Galilee, but at no point does he state or imply that their departure was immediate. One might be inclined to read such an immediate departure into his account had we no reason to contradict it. As it is, John's account makes it clear that they did not return to Galilee for more than a week. Matthew, however, with no intention of mentioning appearances to men in Jerusalem, chooses a convenient form of words which is both accurate and gives continuity to his story.

Matthew and Mark had clearly stated that Jesus was going ahead of his disciples to Galilee and that they would meet him there. One expects to hear at this point that they responded with eagerness and left at once. Matthew, it is true, says quite simply that they 'went to Galilee', though without saying just when. But Mark's gospel (shorter or longer) says nothing at all about any journey to Galilee and confines its story to brief accounts of appearances in and around Jerusalem. He, however, makes it clear that he knew about an appearance in Galilee because he quotes the angel's message, 'He is going before you to Galilee; there you will see him, as he told you.' This is no proof, as some have supposed that Mark intended to write about Galilean appearances and that he probably included such in his now lost ending. He may simply have let slip a detail which corroborates Matthew and John. Luke also takes the reader right through from Easter Sunday evening to the Ascension morning without a hint of any departure from Jerusalem. Furthermore, at that point he says, 'Stay in the city, until you are clothed with power from on high.' He shows in his second book at Acts 1:3 that the account in the gospel is highly condensed and that what might appear to have taken place in a single day was in fact spread over forty days and that Jesus presented himself alive by *many* proofs. He does not, however, say anything about appearances in Galilee. How is Luke to be reconciled with Matthew and John?

K. Bornhäuser tried to reconcile Matthew with Mark and Luke by suggesting that 'Galilee' was in fact a location on the Mount of Olives, so named because it was the regular place of encampment of Galilean pilgrims.[6] This, however, really solves nothing, for it is intrinsically improbable that the Galilean disciples would stay in Jerusalem for forty days, and John 21 explicitly denies it. Also, as the nine disciples at Bethany were already at a point on the far side of this 'Galilee' from the place where Jesus rose, he could hardly be described as going ahead of them to reach it. So Galilee must be given its ordinary meaning, and it must be assumed that Mark and Luke said nothing about appearances in Galilee because it was outside their purpose to do so.

The apparent tardiness of the apostles in responding to the angelic message is more of a problem. The key to the angel's message is to be found in the incident on Maundy Thursday evening, when:

> They went out to the Mount of Olives. Then Jesus said to them, "You will all fall away because of me this night; for it is written, 'I will strike the shepherd, and the sheep of the flock will be scattered.' But after I am raised up, I will go before you to Galilee."

So the angel says:

> He is going before you to Galilee; there you will see him, *as he told you.*[7]

The message is a deliberate recollection of this saying of Jesus, which is to be taken in its full and natural sense. The Shepherd has indeed been smitten (as he said), and he has been raised (as he said), and he is going ahead of you into Galilee to regather his flock (as he said). This did not imply that the only appearances were to be in Galilee, nor that the disciples were to leave immediately. Indeed to leave immediately would have been quite contrary to what was expected of a devout Jew, who in the ordinary way would stay in Jerusalem to observe the six days of unleavened bread which followed the feast of the Passover, and the disciples evidently did not understand the angel's message to mean that. The fact that they did not go to Galilee until the whole festival was over may account for Matthew's reticence about when they went; their stay for a further week is spelled out in John's explicit narrative. Even the Lord's words to the women recorded by Matthew, 'Proclaim to my brethren that they are to go to Galilee, and there they will see me', are more the announcement of a thrilling promise than the issuing of a precise command. Both announcements implied that the divine triumph had begun and that Galilee was to be the place where the scattered army was to re-form its ranks.

When Jesus had disappeared the women hurried on to Bethany to tell their tale and presumably Matthew gives in succinct form his own recollection of that memorable morning: the departure of the other Mary and her companion in the early hours, followed by her return with the report which she gave of the encounter first with the angel and then with Jesus himself. That was how Matthew heard it and that is how he recalled it ever after.

THE APPEARANCE TO CLEOPAS

The next appearance is alluded to in Mark 16:12, which says:

> After this he appeared in another form to two of them, as they were walking into the country.

But Luke tells the full story:

> That very day two of them were going to a village named Emmaus, about seven miles from Jerusalem, and talking with each other about all these things that had happened. While they were talking and discussing together, Jesus himself drew near and went with them. But their eyes were kept from recognising him. And he said to them, "What is this conversation which you are holding with each other as you walk?" And they stood still, looking sad. Then one of them, named Cleopas, answered him, "Are you the only visitor to Jerusalem who does not know the things that have happened there in these days?" And he said to them, "What things?" And they said to him, "Concerning Jesus of Nazareth, who was a prophet mighty in deed and word before God and all the people, and how our chief priests and rulers delivered him up to be condemned to death, and crucified him. But we had hoped that he was the one to redeem Israel. Yes, and besides all this, it is now the third day since this happened.

Moreover, some women of our company amazed us. They were at the tomb early in the morning and did not find his body; and they came back saying that they had even seen a vision of angels, who said that he was alive. Some of those who were with us went to the tomb, and found it just as the women had said; but him they did not see. And he said to them, "O foolish men, and slow of heart to believe all that the prophets have spoken! Was it not necessary that the Christ should suffer these things and enter into his glory?" And beginning with Moses and all the prophets, he interpreted to them in all the scriptures the things concerning himself.

So they drew near to the village to which they were going. He appeared to be going further, but they constrained him, saying, "Stay with us, for it is toward evening and the day is now far spent." So he went in to stay with them. When he was at table with them, he took the bread and blessed, and broke it, and gave it to them. And their eyes were opened and they recognised him; and he vanished out of their sight.

(Luke 24:13–31)

We have already given reasons for identifying Cleopas with Clopas, brother of Joseph of Nazareth, and for locating him in the house of his Zebedee relatives in Jerusalem. He would have witnessed the comings and goings of Mary Magdalene, Peter and John, and the other women, including his wife, Mary. This is borne out by the details of Luke's account. Cleopas says that 'some women of our company ... had ... seen a vision of angels, who said that he was alive;' Luke had also already mentioned that Peter had run to the tomb and seen the linen cloths; he now lets slip his knowledge that Peter was not the only man there by quoting Cleopas as saying, 'Some (plural) of those who were with us (in the same house) went to the tomb.' He then adds, 'But him they did not see', which seems to suggest that they had heard not only the report about angels, but also the unmentionably fantastic tale of Mary Magdalene that she had actually seen Jesus.

As to the unnamed companion of Cleopas, we are left to speculate. It is my own belief (of no importance to this study) that he was Luke himself and that the empty house to which they went in Emmaus was his.[8] This story is one of the most vivid narratives in the whole Bible. C.S. Lewis maintained that 'the whole technique' of 'novelistic, realistic narrative' is a modern invention, which when found in the ancient world means reportage 'pretty close up to the facts'.[9] This account must have come first-hand from Cleopas or his companion. It is interesting to note that it is Cleopas, who had been so closely in touch with the events in John's house, who speaks first to Jesus about what had happened.

Luke's 'village named Emmaus, about seven miles (sixty *stadia*) from Jerusalem' is difficult to identify. A number of Emmaus's are known in Palestine. Eusebius identified it with ᶜAmwas, which is about fourteen and a half miles to the west of Jerusalem, and some manuscripts have been amended from sixty *stadia* to a hundred and sixty accordingly.[10] But apart from the distance being wrong, ᶜAmwas was a town rather than a village. It is better to look for a site nearer the city, but remembering that the village may have entirely disappeared. 'Emmaus' means a place of warm springs, and the village might possibly therefore have had a reputation as a place of healing.

As the two men talked, Jesus came up behind them and joined them. They unburdened their perplexities to him and he set their hearts pounding as he opened up to them the wonders of the Old Testament prophecies. But 'their eyes were kept from recognis-

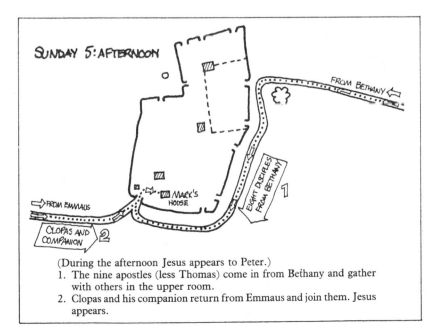

(During the afternoon Jesus appears to Peter.)
1. The nine apostles (less Thomas) come in from Bethany and gather with others in the upper room.
2. Clopas and his companion return from Emmaus and join them. Jesus appears.

ing him' until the breaking of bread, at which time 'their eyes
were opened and they recognised him.' It seems to be characteristic of the early resurrection appearances that Jesus was not
immediately and fully recognised. It was true of Mary in the
garden, of the eleven in the upper room and of the seven in the
fishing boat. It is probably idle to discuss whether it was due to a
change in Jesus' appearance, as Mark 16:12 indicates, or due to
an inhibition in the disciples themselves, as Luke here suggests.
It may well have been something of both. The New Testament
depicts throughout an element of continuity and an element of
discontinuity between Jesus' body before and after the resurrection. Equally it suggests that recognition of Jesus can be
hindered in those who are "slow of heart to believe".

When they reached Emmaus it was 'toward evening', which
need mean no more than 'after noon', the sun being on its way
down. This is insisted upon by K. Bornhäuser; and P. Benoit,
commenting also on the phrase 'the day is far spent', says: 'These
phrases ought not to be taken absolutely literally; it is very
characteristic of Eastern hospitality to ask guests to stay – "Night
is falling, you can start out again tomorrow" – even if it is no later
than two in the afternoon.'[11] We should perhaps think of the
Emmaus disciples as preparing a late midday meal and then after
Jesus had vanished walking back the seven miles up to Jerusalem. Reaching the city before the gates closed at nightfall they
arrive to find the other disciples gathered for their evening meal.

CHAPTER 9

Later that Day and the Sunday Following

THE APPEARANCE TO PETER

Luke continues the story:

> They said to each other, "Did not our hearts burn within us while he talked to us on the road, while he opened to us the scriptures?" And they rose that same hour and returned to Jerusalem; and they found the eleven gathered together and those who were with them, who said, "The Lord has risen indeed, and has appeared to Simon!" Then they told what had happened on the road, and how he was known to them in the breaking of the bread.
>
> *(Luke 24:32–35)*

Mark's short notice is rather different:

> They went back and told the rest, but they did not believe them.
>
> *(Mark 16:11)*

While Cleopas and his friend were engaged in their long walk to Emmaus and back, there must have been eager consultations amongst those they left behind. One can imagine that the nine at Bethany were bewildered yet considerably heartened by what they had heard. They could not really believe the women's story, but neither could they ignore it. They must obviously consult with Peter and John and the others who had been at the centre of affairs. Perhaps Peter's brother Andrew and John's brother James the Elder went into the city for a top-level discussion. In any case it was agreed that all should meet and share an evening meal together in the upper room.

When Cleopas and his companion got back to the city they went straight to John Mark's house and found the meal in progress.[1] They sat behind locked doors, still apprehensive of the attentions of the Jewish authorities. When the Emmaus disciples arrive, they are greeted with the remarkable news, 'The Lord has risen indeed, and has appeared to Simon!' This confident-sounding affirmation about Simon Peter seems to contradict the statement of Mark that their report was greeted with unbelief, though it should be noted that Luke himself says shortly afterwards that even with Jesus present, 'they still disbelieved for joy.'

This allusive reference to an appearance to Peter, is confirmed by Paul's direct statement, 'He appeared to Cephas' (referring to him by the Aramaic form of the name which Jesus gave him). This appearance comes first in Paul's list, though he is careful not to say that it was the first time that Jesus was seen by anyone. Mark had given a hint that Jesus had something special in mind for Peter when he recalled the instructions to the women that they were to 'tell his disciples *and Peter.*' But the gospels are completely silent as to where this meeting took place or as to what occurred at it. Being an appearance to Peter alone, it would not have been in a crowded city house; it could hardly have been in Joseph's garden, which had become a centre of interest to both Jewish and Roman authorities and which lay near a busy thoroughfare. Perhaps he had slipped out by the city gate near John's house and had returned to the solitude of Gethsemane? It must have been an occasion of great poignancy, when the Lord spoke the word of forgiveness to the one who had three times disowned him — an occasion perhaps too personal and too sacred to be made a matter of public knowledge. In John 21 we have a later scene where Peter in the presence of some of his colleagues is restored to his position as leader of the eleven with a thrice-repeated charge to feed Jesus' flock.

How are we to take Luke's affirmation concerning the belief of the disciples and Mark's assertion about their unbelief?[2] The truth must surely be that the ten apostles present were in various states of part-belief and part-unbelief. When the women first told their story they were doubtless greeted with incredulity, both in Jerusalem and in Bethany. But John's faith had begun to recover when he saw the grave-cloths, and the Emmaus disciples had clearly not totally dismissed the women's reports. Peter had come to believe through his meeting with Jesus during the afternoon, but one may imagine that it was a very subdued and scarcely articulate Peter that reported to the others. When Cleopas and his friend told their tale, it added further fuel to Peter's claim, but the apostles' unbelief (momentarily intensified by the terror of the sudden apparition) was finally overcome only by seeing and sitting with and talking to Jesus himself.

This raises the general question of the relation between the faith of the disciples and the appearance of Jesus. It is often said that it was those with expectant faith who saw Jesus. The gospel accounts indicate just the opposite. While there is no evidence that Jesus appeared to any unbeliever, there is abundant evidence that he appeared to disciples who were *not* in a state of eager expectation and who did *not* quickly believe that it was he.[3]

THE FIRST APPEARANCE TO THE TWELVE

Two quite different accounts of what happened next are given by Luke and John. Luke says:

> As they were saying this, Jesus himself stood among them. But they were startled and frightened, and supposed that they saw a spirit. And he said to them, "Why are you troubled, and why do questionings rise in your hearts? See my hands and my feet, that it is I myself; handle me, and see; for a spirit has not flesh and bones as you see that I have." And while they still disbelieved for joy, and wondered, he said to them, "Have you anything here to eat?" They gave him a piece of broiled fish, and he took it and ate before them.
>
> *(Luke 24:36–43)*

John says:

> On the evening of that day, the first day of the week, the doors being shut where the disciples were, for fear of the Jews, Jesus came and stood among them and said to them, "Peace be with you." When he had said this, he showed them his hands and his side. Then the disciples were glad when they saw the Lord. Jesus said to them again, "Peace be with you. As the Father has sent me, even so I send you." And when he had said this, he breathed on them, and said to them, "Receive the Holy Spirit. If you forgive the sins of any, they are forgiven; if you retain the sins of any, they are retained."
>
> *(John 20:19–23)*

Paul follows his mention of the appearance to Cephas, by:

Then to the twelve.

(1 Corinthians 15:5)

It is in fact clear from John that two of the twelve, Judas Iscariot and Thomas, were not there, and from Luke that there were others present in addition. Luke calls them 'the eleven ... and those who were with them.' John uses the expression 'the twelve' in verse 24, but here he uses the term 'disciples', referring to the wider company which Luke describes. It is evident that Paul's use of 'the twelve' and Luke's use of 'the eleven' are ways of referring to the apostolic body collectively, rather than exact numerical computations. Paul may in fact be telescoping two successive appearances, neither of which was precisely to the twelve, since his next reference is to a far larger gathering.

Putting the two accounts together, it seems that before Clopas had finished telling his story and without the doors being opened, Jesus suddenly appeared standing among them. He greeted them: 'Peace be with you.' They were startled and frightened, thinking they had seen a ghost. He gently reproached them for their unbelief and dullness of understanding. 'Why are you so perturbed?' he said. 'Why do questionings arise in your minds? Look at my hands and feet. It is I myself. Touch me and see; no ghost has flesh and bones as you can see that I have.' He then showed them not only his hands and feet, but he drew aside his clothes and showed them the wound in his side. They were still not quite convinced, still wondering, for it seemed too good to be true. Jesus then broke the tension and said to them in matter of fact tones, 'Have you anything here to eat?' They gave him a piece of fish, which he took and unhurriedly ate before their eyes.

Both Luke and John stress the materiality of Jesus. He could be handled, he had flesh and bones and he ate in their presence. Nonetheless his body was a transformed body, which could appear and disappear at will and pass through locked doors and could be levitated contrary to gravity. Yet it was not a new body, but the old buried body in a new form, still capable of eating boiled fish. God's new creation was not a fresh creation *ex nihilo*, but a transmutation of the old.

Luke at this point leaps ahead and spans the whole fifty day period from Easter to Pentecost in ten verses. His two concluding paragraphs begin according to the RSV. '*Then* he said to them ...' and '*Then* he led them out ....' These '*thens*' give a much sharper suggestion of chronological continuity than the Greek justifies. The paragraphs are linked by a weak connective non-temporal particle (*de*) which would be better left untranslated. It seems best to regard Luke as laying side by side (a) a highly condensed account of Jesus' teaching and of the disciples' growing understanding during the period which began that day with the opening of their minds to the scriptures, and which ended on Ascension Day with the command to await their enduement with power (44–49); (b) a short account of the ascension and of the conduct of the disciples in the days immediately following (50–53). He is not packing into one day or even into one day and one night all the events between resurrection and ascension, as his fuller account in Acts 1 shows.

Doubtless, however, Jesus began there and then (as Luke says) to recall the teaching he had given them about the necessity for the fulfilment of the prophecies concerning him in the Old Testament, and their hitherto uncomprehending minds began to understand. He outlined to them the gospel which was to be proclaimed to the world — that the Messiah suffered and rose, and that forgiveness of sins was to be offered in his name to all who repent. He then (as John says) reasserted their status as his witnesses: 'Peace be with you. As the Father has sent me, even so I send you.' He breathed on them, symbolising the Breath of God which they were to receive and in whose power they were to preach the gospel. Through the Spirit they would bring forgiveness to those who accepted the word of forgiveness; through the Spirit they would bring condemnation to those who refused it.

THE SECOND APPEARANCE TO THE TWELVE

John resumes the story:

> Now Thomas, one of the twelve, called the Twin, was not with them when Jesus came. So the other disciples told him, "We have seen the

Lord." But he said to them, "Unless I see in his hands the print of the nails, and place my finger in the mark of the nails, and place my hand in his side, I will not believe."

Eight days later, his disciples were again in the house, and Thomas was with them. The doors were shut, but Jesus came and stood among them, and said, "Peace be with you." Then he said to Thomas, "Put your finger here, and see my hands; and put out your hand, and place it in my side; do not be faithless but believing." Thomas answered him, "My Lord and my God!" Jesus said to him, "Have you believed because you have seen me? Blessed are those who have not seen and yet believe."

(John 20:24–29)

Matthew tells of only one appearance to men, and that in Galilee, while Mark's and Luke's gospels tell only of appearances in or near Jerusalem and do so without any suggestion that they extended over a considerable period of time. John now shows that the eleven remained in Jerusalem for at least eight days before returning to Galilee. It would have been normal in any case for pilgrims to stay on for the six days of unleavened bread which followed the passover.

The next incident has Thomas' 'I will not believe' as its central theme. In earlier glimpses of him in the gospel of John we see Thomas to be a man of ardour, prepared to die for Jesus, and a man of an enquiring mind, ready to voice his incomprehension.[4] Later tradition (apparently well founded) shows him as a missionary of great power, who established churches in India and possibly in Parthia.[5] Could it be that Thomas' supposedly extreme scepticism was in reality an expression of a deeper understanding of the issues than that of his colleagues? Perhaps he more clearly than anyone else realised that the whole thing — message from an angel, supposed sightings of Jesus, supposed touchings of him and talk with him — was either one colossal hallucination, *or* it was much, much more than just resurrection. It not only showed Jesus to be Messiah, it not only showed him to be The Son of God (whatever that exalted term might mean), it showed the utterly incredible: that Jesus was God. Such a belief could only be justified on the most tangible, inescapable evidence: 'Unless I see in his hands the print of the nails, and place my finger in the mark of the nails, and place my hand in his side, I will not believe.' In the event as soon as Jesus spoke to him the issue was decided. He for the first time made explicit what had long been implicit in Jesus' teaching. He made the ultimate Christian confession: 'My Lord and my God!'

CHAPTER 10

In Galilee

BY THE LAKESIDE: A THIRD APPEARANCE TO DISCIPLES

The Passover festival being completed and having spent eight days within walking distance of Golgotha and of Joseph's empty grave, the eleven were evidently told by Jesus to return to their home country in the north. Leaving Jerusalem with all its grim and glorious recollections behind, they probably set out on the Monday. On Wednesday they found themselves back in the down-to-earth surroundings of their lakeside homes in Galilee. With no particular commission to fulfil, Peter got the urge to go fishing again after all these months. Seven of them agreed to take a boat out for a night of deep-sea fishing, but it proved to be a night of fruitless toil.

John tells the whole story:

> After this Jesus revealed himself again to the disciples by the Sea of Tiberias; and he revealed himself in this way. Simon Peter, Thomas called the Twin, Nathanael of Cana in Galilee, the sons of Zebedee, and two others of his disciples were together. Simon Peter said to them, "I am going fishing." They said to him, "We will go with you." They went out and got into the boat; but that night they caught nothing.
>
> Just as day was breaking, Jesus stood on the beach; yet the disciples did not know that it was Jesus. Jesus said to them, "Children, have you any fish?" They answered him, "No". He said

to them, "Cast the net on the right side of the boat, and you will find some." So they cast it, and now they were not able to haul it in, for the quantity of fish. That disciple whom Jesus loved said to Peter, "It is the Lord!" When Simon Peter heard that it was the Lord, he put on his clothes, for he was stripped for work, and sprang into the sea. But the other disciples came in the boat, dragging the net full of fish, for they were not far from the land, but about a hundred yards off.

When they got out on land, they saw a charcoal fire there, with fish lying on it, and bread. Jesus said to them, "Bring some of the fish that you have just caught." So Simon Peter went aboard and hauled the net ashore, full of large fish, a hundred and fifty-three of them; and although there were so many, the net was not torn. Jesus said to them, "Come and have breakfast." Now none of the disciples dared ask him, "Who are you?" They knew it was the Lord. Jesus came and took the bread and gave it to them, and so with the fish. This was now the third time that Jesus was revealed to the disciples after he was raised from the dead.

When they had finished breakfast, Jesus said to Simon Peter, "Simon, son of John, do you love me more than these?" He said to him, "Yes, Lord; you know that I love you." He said to him, "Feed my lambs." A second time he said to him, "Simon, son of John, do you love me?" He said to him, "Yes, Lord; you know that I love you." He said to him, "Tend my sheep". He said to him the third time, "Simon, son of John, do you love me?" Peter was grieved because he said to him the third time, "Do you love me?" And he said to him, "Lord, you know everything; you know that I love you." Jesus said to him, "Feed my sheep. Truly, truly, I say to you, when you were young, you girded yourself and walked where you would; but when you are old, you will stretch out your hands, and another will gird you and carry you where you do not wish to go." (This he said to show by what death he was to glorify God.) And after this he said to him, "Follow me."

Peter turned and saw following them the disciple whom Jesus loved, who had lain close to his breast at the supper and had said, "Lord, who is it that is going to betray you?" When Peter saw him, he said to Jesus, "Lord, what about this man?" Jesus said to him, "If it is my will that he remain until I come, what is that to you? Follow me!" The saying spread abroad among the brethren that this disciple was not to die; yet Jesus did not say to him that he was not to die, but, "If it is my will that he remain until I come, what is that to you?"

This is the disciple who is bearing witness to these things, and who has written these things; and we know that his testimony is true.

But there are also many other things which Jesus did; were every one of them to be written, I suppose that the world itself could not contain the books that would be written.

(John 21)

When John declares this to be the third revelation of Jesus to the disciples after he was raised from the dead, it is not to be taken as implying ignorance of his individual appearance to Peter or of his appearance to Cleopas and his friend, but it refers to collective appearances to the apostles. Jesus now showed himself again in new surroundings and in a quite unhurried way as they talked and ate round a fire on the beach. One of the purposes of this appearance was the further rehabilitation of Peter as leader of the apostles, another was the countering of the saying that the beloved disciple was not to die. A third purpose is suggested by the next event which was to take place.

THE GREAT RECOMMISSIONING

In Paul's list of appearances of Jesus to his commissioned followers there comes next:

Then he appeared to more than five hundred brethren at one time, most of whom are still alive.

(I Corinthians 15:6)

The importance of this meeting is emphasized by the very large number present. There is no point in the forty days where a *chance* gathering of 500 brethren can be plausibly imagined. It could not have been near Jerusalem at passover time, for John sets out the first three appearances to the apostles in detail: there were appearances in the same house on successive Sundays in or near Jerusalem and then (after the pilgrims had dispersed) an appearance to a group of just seven disciples by the lakeside in Galilee. John declares specifically that this last 'was now the third time that Jesus was revealed to the disciples'. Therefore the meeting with the 500 must have been later than this and after the dispersal of the festival crowds. (It should be noted also that even if such a chance gathering could be conceived, it would not have been composed exclusively of 'brethren', as many of the Galilean pilgrims were not believers in Jesus.) It is even more difficult to imagine such a large concourse chancing to assemble in Galilee and virtually impossible that it should consist only of believers. It could not of course have been at the next great festival in Jerusalem, which was Pentecost, since this was ten days after Jesus' last appearance. So the meeting with 500 brethren must have been a *convened* meeting.

This means that it was probably the one in Galilee upon which Matthew lays such stress:

> Now the eleven disciples went to Galilee, to the mountain to which Jesus had directed them. And when they saw him they worshipped him; but some doubted. And Jesus came and said to them, "All authority in heaven and on earth has been given to me. Go therefore and make disciples of all nations, baptizing them in the name of the Father and of the Son and of the Holy Spirit, teaching them to observe all that I have commanded you; and lo, I am with you always, to the close of the age."
>
> *(Matthew 28:16–20)*

Although this one in Galilee is the only appearance to men mentioned by Matthew, his wording contains a hint of an earlier meeting: 'The eleven disciples went ... to the mountain to which Jesus directed them.' Thus far Matthew has spoken only of the *angel's* message that they were to see Jesus at an unspecified place in Galilee. Now he speaks of *the* mountain to which *Jesus* had directed them. This specific direction could of course have come from Jesus through the angel without Matthew saying so, but given our knowledge of meetings of apostles with Jesus from the other gospels, it seems likely that he was thinking of an occasion at which Jesus himself told them precisely where and when to assemble. As will be seen presently, there had to be an element of secrecy about the Galilee meeting, which would have made the delivery of such a message at secondhand by the women at the very earliest stage unlikely. The meeting with the seven fishermen on the shores of the Lake of Galilee described by John provides a likely occasion for Jesus to have given them their instructions. That he directed them to a location in the Galilean hills suggests that the assembly was not to be a small one, for a dozen or more could easily have met privately indoors.

Mark does not record this meeting, but he implies it, and implies its great importance, when he records the message to the women: 'he is going before you to Galilee; there you will see him, as he told you.' Although neither Matthew nor Mark give any hint of a large gathering, Matthew does indicate the presence of others besides the apostles. He says: 'When they saw him they worshipped him; but some doubted.' The only men specifically referred to here are 'the eleven', who are said to have 'worshipped him'. Matthew goes on to say, '*but some* doubted'. Does this mean that some of the apostles doubted? His precise form of words at this point needs to be noted. The nearest parallel is in Matthew 26:67, where it says, 'Then they spat in his face, and struck him; *and some* slapped him.' The Greek construction which is used here normally signifies a change of subject, and the standard grammar translates it at both points 'but others'.[1] In neither case does the language *demand* that those mentioned in the first part of the sentence and the 'others' mentioned in the second part should be regarded as completely mutually exclusive, but it is natural to take them as referring to different groups. It would mean that 'some others *of those present* doubted', but not the apostles.

This is of course borne out if we take the other gospels into consideration. If John's account is true, Matthew was present on two occasions when Jesus appeared to the apostles in Jerusalem, and he knew that the apostles' doubts were stilled before they left for Galilee. Therefore, if Matthew is the source of those words, those whom he describes as doubting could hardly have been apostles (unless he is referring merely to some momentary hesitation — which would scarcely have been worth mentioning). But if Paul's mention of an appearance to 500 brethren after the appearance to 'the twelve' refers to this same meeting in Galilee, it would mean that many others were present. It is evidently no part of Matthew's plan to write either about the experiences of the men in Jerusalem or about the experiences of the wider company of believers in Galilee. But he chooses a form of words which neatly describes the faith of the eleven and hints at the presence of others with doubts.

This meeting was for the 'brethren',[2] that is to say, for the 'disciples' of Jesus in the broad sense of that term. It was no mean feat to gather so large a company without rousing the curiosity of unbelieving neighbours. It must have been necessary for Jesus to give rather precise instructions to a small group of leaders if it was to be accomplished. At this point John's contribution fits neatly in. Jesus appeared to seven of the leading disciples and it was they presumably who organised the great assembly. It must have been an absorbing undertaking to list the villages of Galilee and to recall the committed believers in each place, and then to arrange for them all to be informed without arousing the suspicions of neighbours or of Herod's agents.

With so many people involved, the fact that some doubted is not surprising, since there must inevitably have been considerable differences of temperament and of spiritual discernment among them. Matthew was evidently right to stress the importance of this Galilean meeting. Although the post-resurrection witness was to begin in Jerusalem, the strength of the Christian movement lay in Jesus' native Galilee, and it was his purpose to regather and to recommission his scattered army there. This great assembly was quite unlike any of the other meetings and it had a unique place in providing a strong base in the church as a whole for the resurrection faith. It is interesting to note that in Jesus' final charge to the eleven, he makes no mention of Galilee. He describes their sphere of witness as 'in Jerusalem and in all Judea and Samaria and to the end of the earth'. Is this perhaps because by then 'Galilee of the Gentiles' (as Matthew calls it)[3] already had hundreds of commissioned witnesses? Matthew may have seen his record of the Great Commission as an encouragement to the members of the Jerusalem church who had been forcibly scattered by persecution to view their dispersion as a God-sent opportunity to get on with the task.

When the great day came they quietly gathered in their hundreds on a remote mountain-side to await their risen Lord. As in the case of the appearance to the women, Jesus seems to have approached them from a distance. The eleven evidently recognized him at once and prostrated themselves in worship. Some of the others, though fully aware that Jesus had risen, were slower to let themselves believe that the approaching figure was really he. The reference to doubts provides a background for the great words of encouragement which are to follow. As on previous occasions his appearance was unhurried, so that all the five hundred who were present might have no temptation to think of it later as an hallucination. He repeated again what he had said to the eleven. He spoke of his relation to the Father and of the coming of the Spirit and he commissioned them to go into all the world to make disciples of all nations. They were to proclaim the good news and to warn of judgment to come. They were to baptize in the name of the Father, Son and Spirit. They were to teach obedience to his commands. He promised his presence with them to the end of the age. So it was that he recommissioned his apostles, along with a great army of faithful witnesses, who were to form the vanguard of the worldwide church.

THE APPEARANCE TO JAMES

Paul continues:

> Then he appeared to James.
>
> (*I Corinthians 15:7*)

This appearance is mentioned nowhere in the gospels. It was to a James who evidently was not one of the twelve, for there is no suggestion that either James son of Zebedee, who was killed by Herod in AD 42 or James the younger, of whom we hear no more, had any special leadership role to fill in the church. James 'the Lord's brother', however rose to prominence as head of the church in Jerusalem after Peter was imprisoned, and is mentioned in Acts and in Paul's Epistle to the Galatians,[4] and is agreed to be almost certainly the one to whom Paul refers. The relatives of Jesus are discussed in Appendix III, and reasons are given for believing that James was the eldest of four boys born to Joseph and Mary after the birth of Jesus. Though younger than Jesus, he was brought up with him, but evidently without knowledge of the special circumstances of Jesus' birth. To accept one's own brother (however greatly admired) as the divine Son would require a painful revolution.

We may assume that Jesus' appearance to him (like the appearance to Peter) was a very personal affair. It took place after the meeting with the 500 and before Ascension Day, which was about ten days before Pentecost, which would have been the next festival to bring the Galileans to Jerusalem, so it probably took place in their home country in Galilee. Once again the narratives dovetail. John tells us that the brothers did not believe and that at the time of the crucifixion the Lord's mother was not committed to their care, but to his. But by the time of the Ascension six weeks later we find the Lord's brothers praying with the apostles.[5] Maybe they all mingled inconspicuously with the crowd that met him in the mountain of Galilee, and later Jesus appeared again to James privately. James, for all his rectitude and sincerity, had evidently never yielded faith to Jesus during his ministry. Now he must have felt grievously the shame of having lived so close to him so long, yet in unbelief. Jesus forgave him and restored him and prepared him for eventual leadership of the Jerusalem church. The change wrought in James was so complete that he eventually came to write of himself as a 'slave of Jesus Christ'.[6] Paul may well have heard firsthand about the appearances to Peter and to James when he went to Jerusalem three years after his conversion.[7]

CHAPTER 11

Farewell

The end of the story is told us by three writers. Paul says:

Then to all the apostles (1 Corinthians 15:7).

Mark 16:15–20 says:

> And he said to them, "Go into all the world and preach the gospel to the whole creation. He who believes and is baptized will be saved; but he who does not believe will be condemned. And these signs will accompany those who believe: in my name they will cast out demons; they will speak in new tongues; they will pick up serpents, and if they drink any deadly thing, it will not hurt them; and they will lay their hands on the sick; and they will recover."
>
> So then the Lord·Jesus, after he had spoken to them, was taken up into heaven, and sat down at the right hand of God. And they went forth and preached everywhere, while the Lord worked with them and confirmed the message by the signs that attended it. Amen.

Luke in his gospel says:

> Then he said to them, "These are my words which I spoke to you, while I was still with you, that everything written about me in the law of Moses and the prophets and the psalms must be fulfilled." Then he opened their minds to understand the scriptures, and said to them, "Thus it is written, that the Christ should suffer and on the third day rise from the dead, and that repentance and forgiveness of sins should be preached in his name to all nations, beginning from Jerusalem. You are witnesses of these things. And behold, I send the

promise of my Father upon you; but stay in the city, until you are clothed with power from on high."

Then he led them out as far as Bethany, and lifting up his hands he blessed them. While he blessed them, he parted from them. And they returned to Jerusalem with great joy, and were continually in the temple blessing God.

In chapter 1 of the Acts of the Apostles he writes:

In the first book, O Theophilus, I have dealt with all that Jesus began to do and teach, until the day when he was taken up, after he had given commandment through the Holy Spirit to the apostles whom he had chosen. To them he presented himself alive after his passion by many proofs, appearing to them during forty days, and speaking of the kingdom of God. And while staying with them he charged them not to depart from Jerusalem, but to wait for the promise of the Father, which, he said, "You heard from me, for John baptized with water, but before many days you shall be baptized with the Holy Spirit."

So when they had come together, they asked him, "Lord, will you at this time restore the kingdom to Israel?" He said to them, "It is not for you to know times or seasons which the Father has fixed by his own authority. But you shall receive power when the Holy Spirit has come upon you; and you shall be my witnesses in Jerusalem and in all Judea and Samaria and to the end of the earth." And when he had said this, as they were looking on, he was lifted up, and a cloud took him out of their sight. And while they were gazing into heaven as he went, behold, two men stood by them in white robes, and said, "Men of Galilee, why do you stand looking into heaven? This Jesus, who was taken up from you into heaven, will come in the same way as you saw him go into heaven."

Then they returned to Jerusalem from the mount called Olivet, which is near Jerusalem, a sabbath day's journey away; and when they had entered, they went up to the upper room, where they were staying, Peter and John and James and Andrew, Philip and Thomas, Bartholomew and Matthew, James the son of Alphaeus and Simon the Zealot and Judas the son of James. All these with one accord devoted themselves to prayer, together with the women and Mary the mother of Jesus, and with his brothers.

Subsequently he quotes Paul as saying:

For many days he appeared to those who came up with him from Galilee to Jerusalem, who are now his witnesses to the people (13:31).

According to Paul and according to Acts 1:2 this final appearance was to the apostles. The term 'apostle' is occasionally used
of others than the twelve, but it seems most likely that the
reference here is to the remaining eleven, who are in fact named
in Acts 1:13. They had evidently been given instructions to go
back to Mark's house[1] in Jerusalem to wait for the final event
which were to prepare them for their world mission. In the
gospel Luke tells how Jesus led them out of the city towards
Bethany and in Acts how they afterwards returned from Olivet to
Jerusalem. Olivet, he says, was a sabbath day's journey from the
city. For twelve men to have undertaken such an expedition
without exciting attention, it seems probable that they left early
in the morning before the sun was up. This would mean that any
prior talk with Jesus would have taken place during the hours of
darkness.

So maybe it was Wednesday evening, with the disciples once
more gathered together behind closed doors in the upper room,
that Jesus again stood among them. Not frightened, but relaxed
and eager, they talked the night through.

The account in Mark spans the whole period from Easter
Sunday to Ascension Day. The commission which he records is
introduced by '*And* he said to them....' This 'and' is translated
'then' in the New English Bible, so placing this commission at
the Easter Sunday meal in the upper room. But this is to read far
too much into Mark's story. The 'and' does not necessarily tie
what follows to what has gone before. In fact it is quite a habit of
Mark to start a new paragraph with an 'and' which in idiomatic
English is often best left untranslated.[2] It would seem best to
regard 15–20 as a single unit, telling of the final instructions to
the eleven immediately before the ascension and of their mighty
preaching afterwards. It is *possible* that Mark's account is an
independent report of the teaching of Jesus on the mountain in
Galilee which Matthew records, but on the whole it seems more
likely not, and this for three reasons. Firstly, Mark's account
does not appear to move outside the Jerusalem area, which (we
have suggested) is because Mark himself did not go up to Galilee.
Secondly, the two accounts in spite of their common thrust have
remarkably little in common verbally — little more than the
word 'Go' and the two closely related words translated 'all'.
Thirdly, the emphasis in Matthew is on the authority of the risen

Christ, while the emphasis in Mark is on the miraculous powers which are to be granted to those who believe. The one seems rather more suitable to those who are just beginning to learn the meaning of the resurrection, the other to those who at the end of the forty days are looking forward to the outpouring of Pentecost.

Luke in his concise conclusion to the first treatise gives no hint of instructions to return to Galilee or of further appearances either there or in Jerusalem, but he simply records that they are to stay in the city until they are clothed with power from on high. In his second treatise, however, he makes it clear that 'he presented himself alive after his passion by many proofs, appearing to them during forty days.'[3] That he should have mentioned only two[4] appearances in the gospel does not mean that he is unaware of others. As Paul's companion he must have known of the six appearances which the apostle mentions in 1 Corinthians 15; and if he knew Mark's gospel he would have known of a promised appearance in Galilee; and if he knew Matthew's he would have known of its fulfilment. Nor is it necessary to suppose that Luke heard new stories between the writing of the two books — he is deliberately telescoping a long and complex series of events.[5]

After Jesus had appeared once more in the upper room the fleeting hours that followed must have been bathed in the bliss of love and trust, the eleven learning yet more of the wonderful purposes of God, and encouraged by the promise of miraculous powers to aid them in their preaching. As dawn began to break and the mists still lay on the ground[6] they left the house and once more followed the fateful route which they had taken on the night of the Last Supper. Jesus led them out of the city gate, down into the Kidron valley, past the Garden of Gethsemane, up the Mount of Olives, and finally 'out as far as Bethany.' 'As far as' translates an unusual expression, which may perhaps be better rendered 'as far as the path to Bethany'. E.F.F. Bishop says that it 'would appear to mean the Mount of Olives at the summit where the descent to Bethany comes into view.'[7] The ascension did not take place at Bethany itself which is nearly two miles from the city, but as Acts says, at 'Olivet, which is near Jerusalem, a sabbath day's journey away' — that is, at a distance of not more than 1,200 yards. The region of the traditional site on the Mount of Olives overlooking the city seems to fit the gospel data.

Their very last words were exchanged on the Mount of Olives, when Jesus warns the apostles not to preoccupy themselves about the time of the restoration of the kingdom and again promises them the power of the Spirit for their worldwide witness. Then 'he was lifted up, and a cloud took him out of their sight.' Luke here seems to suggest that Jesus was enveloped by a passing cloud shortly after leaving the ground and that they did not see him disappearing into the distance on a journey into the upper atmosphere, which literally minded people might have inferred from the longer text of Luke 24:51 or from Mark 16:19.

They returned to the city in great joy knowing that God had given them many irrefutable proofs of their Lord's resurrection. Their doubts were resolved. They now knew who he was — their Lord and their God. They now knew their task — to make him known throughout the world. They now knew the world's great hope — to see him return and reign in glory over a creation transformed by the power which brought him resurrection.

CONCLUSION

Such is the story. Many of the details are of course uncertain. Imagination and reasoned conjecture inevitably play a part in trying to picture things as they were. It is hoped that imagination has been disciplined and that conjecture has been tied closely to the text of the narratives and to the known facts. However uncertain the details, it is submitted that piecing together the different accounts has made it possible to follow with tolerable certainty the main course of events, though of course the full story would have been considerably more complex.

The initial appearances in Jerusalem were clearly important evidentially. There was great psychological value in staying around within walking distance of the empty tomb for eight days, to preclude the possibility of any later suspicion of hallucination. As Paul was later to remind Herod Agrippa, 'This was not done in a corner.'[8] Many, believers and unbelievers, must have come to have a look at Joseph's garden, so that the disappearance of the body became public knowledge which could be confidently appealed to in Jerusalem. It was a solitary grave in a private garden, and everyone knew there could be no mistake of identification. Furthermore, this was not done in a hurry. Time was of the essence of the training. There were 'many proofs', which were to extend eventually over nearly six weeks. Some of them ate with him and talked with him at leisure, and in this way impressions became permanent, and disciples who were strained and bewildered became calm and confident.

During the first fifteen days or so he appeared at least seven times and quietly taught individuals and groups about the kingdom of God, but all this was preparatory to the great gathering in the hills of Galilee. It is this gathering to which Matthew directs almost exclusive attention. He tells the Jerusalem guard episode very fully for apologetic reasons, and then concentrates with great conciseness on the Galilean reconstitution of the Christian movement.

Once his followers had grasped the fact that Jesus had conquered death, they would instinctively have expected him to establish his throne in *Jerusalem* without delay. To counter this reaction, the Maundy Thursday promise and the announcement on the resurrection morning direct their minds instead to *Galilee*. In Galilee the apostles were made the instrument for regathering the scattered believers, and in their presence they were recommissioned. They were re-formed as the leaders of a great company who had become witnesses of the resurrection. In the atmosphere of Galilee they were weaned afresh from the idea of a temporal Jewish Messianic kingdom, till ready to be sent back to the city which had crucified the Lord to begin their worldwide witness.

The forty days wrought an extraordinary transformation in the apostles. At the beginning they had been mere disciples — learners who had completely failed. At the end they had become rulers of a new community. For their new task they had been welded into a unity hard to parallel elsewhere in the history of the world. History records again and again how the death of a great leader is followed by strife and division among those who succeed him. These men had been brought very close together through their common anguish and they remained united when their leader left the scene. Finally they were sent back to the place where Jesus had died, had been buried and had risen to life again, and they were told, 'Behold, I send the promise of my

Father upon you; but stay in the city, until you are clothed with power from on high.' From there a great new programme was to unfold.

Looked at in another way the story is a progressive revelation of the most stunning of all divine interventions in the history of man, made to believers, as they were able to bear it. The believing women were ready to receive the resurrection message sooner than the men. These women saw first an opened tomb, then an empty tomb, then a vision of angels. Then followed the angels' proclamation, and finally Jesus himself met and spoke first to one of them and then to others. Then the men received a series of developing revelations: first they heard the women's story, then saw the empty tomb, then observed the significance of the grave cloths. Then Jesus himself went along with the disciples walking to Emmaus and began to expound to them the meaning of his passion. For a considerable time he kept his identity from them, then momentarily made himself known to them before he vanished from their sight. All this was preparatory to his commissioning of the official witnesses: Peter, the eleven, Thomas, the five hundred and finally his own brother James, who was one day to lead the Jerusalem church. There only remained the last farewell and the waiting for the Spirit's power, which would send them out to turn the world upside down.[9]

So ends an investigation which we believe has shown that the charge of irreconcilability brought against the resurrection stories has not been proved. Rather it has shown that these records exhibit the characteristics of accurate and independent reporting, for superficially they show great disharmony, but on close examination the details gradually fall into place. We have seen how an accurate knowledge of topography, a full acquaintance with the actors in the drama and an understanding of the differing viewpoints of the narrators, all throw light on the probable course of events. Maybe there are problems not fully solved and problems given a wrong solution, but when every effort has been made to give the details of the narratives their full weight, they add up to a consistent story. The imperfect knowledge that we have gained by laborious effort nearly two millenia after the events was of course immediately accessible in a fuller and more accurate form to those who had lived through them. The possession of such knowledge goes far towards explaining the certainty, stability and depth of the faith of the early Christians in their risen Lord.

Glory be to God!

APPENDIX I

Gospel Criticism

It will be found that I give little space to the discussion of source criticism, and even less to form and redaction criticism. This is not because I think them unimportant or illegitimate or valueless when judiciously handled; it is simply because this is not the book in which to deal with them. On the one hand they would demand too much technicality and too much space, and on the other the discussion would in the outcome be largely irrelevant. In the case of source criticism debate still rages around the Synoptic Problem, with the whole field now in a greater state of flux than it has been since the beginning of the century. Much discussion is going on as to whether the writer of Matthew knew Mark's gospel or whether the writer of Mark knew Matthew's or whether indeed neither knew the other. Again, the notion that Matthew and Luke independently used the same Q source or sources is being challenged by a growing number of scholars who think that Luke took his 'Q material' direct from Matthew. In addition, the question of whether John knew one or more of the Synoptists and to what extent his material is of historical worth are matters in current debate. It has been said that he who marries the spirit of this age will be a widower in the next. We should be most unwise to assume the truth of the theories which have recently had the greatest vogue.

Form critics have tended to operate on the unproved supposition that the recounting of the gospel stories changed greatly in form and substance over the years and that the details of those stories are therefore seldom of historical worth – details are mere embroidery, which are not to be taken as serious history. Similarly redaction critics have been inclined to regard changes introduced by one evangelist when using the work of another as being historically suspect and therefore to be discounted. But it is quite gratuitous to assume that because one writer made use of the work of another, his alterations and additions are therefore simply inventions out of his own head. He may have had other good sources of information, in some cases he may even have been an eyewitness. Thus it is clear that much of form and redaction criticism is begging questions which should not be begged.

It is important to realise that the critical procedures which have whittled away the authority of different parts of the gospels are neither infallible nor sacrosanct. It is valuable, even if only as an experimental exercise, to break away from these procedures and to work on the supposition that the evangelists may have got their facts right, and see what happens. This is an exercise which can stand on its own feet without paying much attention to the many critical questions which have been raised and which need answering in their own place.

I should indeed have liked to have presented the whole case in a completely objective manner, without any reference to theories of authorship and date. That is, simply to have set out the facts as stated by the different authors and shown how they fitted together. But harmonization of narratives which totally ignores the standpoints of the authors is bound to some extent to be special pleading. It is only fully convincing if it illuminates the rationale of the various writers. Source criticism is an exciting and important subject and in recent years I have come to believe in very early dates for the gospels and in a view of their interrelation which is extremely traditional.[1] All the main ideas of the book were, however, worked out before I came to these views and they are in fact only marginally affected by theories of authorship. I have tried not to obtrude these theories, but neither have I tried to conceal them, because they seem to throw interesting light on a number of the finer points in the gospel texts.

HARMONISTIC EXEGESIS

It will be noticed that at a number of points I appeal to the evidence from one gospel to throw light on the intended meaning of another. Such harmonistic exegesis is generally frowned on in modern study of the gospels, except in cases where one writer appears to be actually using another gospel in his composition. It is held that each gospel must be considered in its own terms and be allowed to tell its own story and that ideas of one evangelist should not be read into the ideas of another.

This is in general a sound principle. It is particularly so if one regards the gospels as late creations which retain little contact with history. This applies, for instance, if one regards the stories about Jesus as the end-product of long processes of development which took place in widely separated parts of the world. If, on the other hand, we take the gospels to be apostolic in origin (even if not apostolic in actual authorship), and stemming from witnesses who worked together for a good many years and who in many cases participated in the same events, the matter is different. The choice of words of the various evangelists is conditioned by their knowledge of the historical facts, and statements by one evangelist (if true) are bound to limit or fill out the statements made by another. On this principle, the old commentaries which explained one gospel by another, had every justification for doing so. Exegesis cannot be divorced from criticism.

Of course, the individuality of different writers must be respected, and the distinctive aims of different works (where these can be discerned) must be taken into account. Forced harmonizing is worthless. The tendency today, however, is the opposite – to force the New Testament writings into disharmony, in order to emphasize their individuality. The current analytical approach to the gospels often has the effect of making scholars more and more uncertain at more and more points, till eventually their view of Jesus and his teaching is lost in haze. The harmonistic approach, on the other hand, enables one to ponder long and conscientiously over every detail of the narrative and to see how one account illuminates and modifies another. Gradually (without fudging) people and events take shape and grow in solidity and the scenes come to life in one's mind. Such study is beautifully constructive and helps to vindicate the presuppositions on which it is based. It is sad and strange when immense learning leads to little knowledge of the person studied. One thing is certain: Jesus was a concrete, complex and fascinating figure of history, and any method of study which fails to reveal him as such is working on the wrong lines.

The Sinner of Luke 7 and Mary Magdalene of Luke 8

The surprising nature of Luke's insertion at this point of 8:1–3 can be fully seen only if his method of composition in the whole section is examined. In this part of the gospel Luke is broadly speaking following the order of Mark. Apart from a brief crossing to the country of the Gerasenes on the east of the lake, the whole of Mark 2–5 seems to be set near the northern shore of the Sea of Galilee, and with minor exceptions almost the whole of Mark's story is repeated in Luke's gospel. Here are the main incidents:

Mark			Luke	
2:	1–12	Capernaum: paralysed man healed	5:	17–26
	13–17	call of Levi		27–32
	18–22	Question about fasting		33–39
	23–28	Plucking grain	6:	1–5
3:	1–6	Healing of man with a withered hand		6–11
	(7–12	Many healings		17–19)
	13–19	Choosing of the Twelve		12–16
	31–35	Jesus' mother and brothers	8:	19–21
4:	1–34	Parable of sower, etc.		4–18
	35–41	Stilling of the storm		22–25
5:	1–20	Healing of Gerasene demoniac		26–39
	21–43	Healing of Jairus' daughter		40–56

It will be noted that Luke makes some small omissions when he comes to Mark 3:20–30 which he offsets by some large insertions which occupy Luke 6:17 – 8:3. Luke's insertions are:

Sermon on a level place	6:	17–49
Healing of centurion's slave at Capernaum	7:	1–10
Raising of a young man at Nain		11–17
Messengers from John the Baptist		18–35
Anointing by the sinner		36–50
Preaching tour with Mary Magdalene and others	8:	1–3

The sections above in italics have parallels in Matthew; the other sections consist entirely of new matter. Luke clearly intended at this point to incorporate his own version of the Sermon on the Mount and two other major incidents which are also recorded by Matthew, and in addition to give three new items of his own.

Luke's three new items need to be examined in turn.

(1) 7:11. 'Soon afterward' he went to a city called Nain, and his disciples and a great crowd went with him.'
Note:
(a) 'Soon afterward' shows that Luke is interested in the chronology.
(b) The visit was to a town some twenty miles from Capernaum.
(c) On this considerable journey, Jesus was accompanied by disciples and others.
(2) 7:37. Luke mentions 'a woman of the (unspecified) city, a sinner.'
(3) 8:1–3 'Soon afterward he went on through cities and villages, preaching and bringing the good news of the kingdom of God. And the twelve were with him, and also some women who had been healed of evil spirits and infirmities: Mary, called Magdalene, from whom seven demons had gone out, and Joanna, the wife of Chuza, Herod's steward, and Susanna, and many others, who provided for them out of their means.'
Note:
(a) Again there is a chronological reference.
(b) Visits are described which must have included places remote from the lake.
(c) Again there is a considerable journey in which Jesus is accompanied by the twelve and others.
(d) It is followed (Luke 8:4–18) by teaching, which according to Mark (4:1) was given by the lakeside (cf. Luke 8:22), and by other incidents in and around Capernaum, which was Jesus' base of operations.
As far as subject matter is concerned, the logical place to have inserted 8:1–3 would have been *before* the visits to Nain and to the unspecified

city, where it would have fitted admirably. Instead, however, Luke puts its after the story of the sinner-woman and connects the two paragraphs by the chronological note 'soon afterward'. It is exceedingly unlikely that the three women named and the 'many others' all began their ministrations precisely at this point, since Jesus' large party had been itinerating at least as far back as the visit to Nain. If, however, the woman of chapter 7 joined the other women at this point, Luke's connection of thought and hence his order of narration would be explained.

It is curious that I.H. Marshall in his careful and thorough commentary: *The Gospel of Luke* (Paternoster, Exeter, 1978 pp. 315f.) thinks it clear that Luke does not identify Mary Magdalene with the sinner, but he does think that in Luke's *source* the paragraph about the ministering women may have served to show how those who had been healed by Jesus demonstrated their gratitude to him. But if in the gospel's source, why not in the gospel itself?

His further suggestion that this paragraph is included because of Luke's wish 'to show that those who were witnesses of the resurrection of Jesus were the women who had accompanied him from Galilee' is not altogether convincing. Three women are named here and three at 24:10, but, though two of the names (Mary Magdalene and Joanna) are common to both lists, two (Susanna and Mary mother of James) are not. It is very doubtful if the first passage was included sixteen chapters before the second in order to establish the credentials of the latter group of women. It seems more likely that Luke introduced it here with 'Soon after ... ' simply because Mary Magdalene did in fact join the other women at this point.

Part of Luke's purpose is to call attention to the part played by women with money in supporting Jesus and his large following. Mary Magdalene we know came in that category, and Luke adds Susanna to the list. But it is unlikely that Mary mother of James was a woman of means, probably being (as we argue in chapter 3) the wife of Clopas, brother of Joseph the carpenter.

The Mother and Brothers of Jesus

It will have been observed that throughout this discussion the position has been adopted that James, Joses and Simeon, sons of Clopas, are to be distinguished from James, Joses, Simon (and Judas), who are described as 'brothers' of Jesus by the people of Nazareth. It has also been assumed that the 'brothers' of Jesus were children both to Joseph and Mary after the birth of Jesus. As both these points are contested, they deserve further examination.

THEORIES OF RELATIONSHIP

To take the second point first. The most natural reading of the gospels implies that Joseph and Mary enjoyed normal relations after the birth of their 'firstborn', Matthew telling us that Joseph took his wife, 'but knew her not until she had borne a son'.[1] And the most natural reading of the gospel implies that they then had a large family, consisting probably of at least three girls and four more boys.[2] There are sixteen references to Jesus' brothers in the New Testament, with no hint that they were step-brothers or cousins or foster-brothers. The fact that twelve of these references are coupled with a reference to his mother (occasionally with a reference to Joseph) suggests that mother and brothers had an intimate relationship. In the five separate incidents that are recorded there is a strong sense of family solidarity.

This view of Jesus' brothers was first argued in detail by the fourth century scholar Helvidius. At the time the idea (so contrary to the normal Jewish view) was growing that virginity represented a higher state of moral excellence than matrimony. This seems to have led to a desire to show that the gospel teaching was consistent with a belief in the continuing virginity of the Lord's mother. Epiphanius (c. 315–403) was the great advocate of the theory that the 'brothers' were sons of Joseph by a former wife. Jerome (c. 342–420) invented the theory, which was widely accepted throughout the Western church, that the 'brothers' were cousins – on Mary's side. A recent Roman Catholic writer, John McHugh, has argued that the three classical views are all untenable, and holds that at least three 'brothers' were cousins on Joseph's side of the family and that Joseph became foster-father to two of them when their father died.[3]

McHUGH'S THEORY

The theories of Epiphanius and Jerome have been sufficiently examined by McHugh and others, but McHugh's new theory merits consideration. The weight of his argument rests on the premise that unless there is proof to the contrary the James and Joses of the burial narratives must be identified with the James and Joses mentioned earlier in the same gospels. He considers that Matthew's and Mark's mention of the last two 'brothers' of Jesus (Simon and Judas) in a different order may suggest that they were not full blood-brothers of James and Joses, and this in turn may suggest that James and Joses were not blood-brothers of the Lord.

He introduces into the story a new Mary, sister to Joseph and to Clopas, whom he distinguishes from Mary wife of Clopas. He argues that it is a mistake to try to identify too closely the women who watched at a distance with the women who stood by the cross. In particular it is a mistake to identify Mary mother of James and Joses with Mary wife of Clopas. At the cross were (a) Mary *wife* of Clopas and (b) 'the other Mary', who, he conjectures, was *sister* to Clopas. This means that the wife, sister and sister-in-law of Clopas were all named Mary, thus:

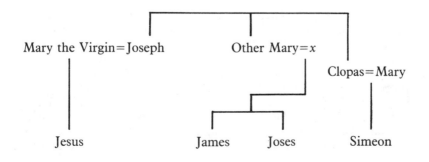

He takes John 19:25 to mean: 'Standing by the cross of Jesus were his mother and his mother's *sister-in-law* and Mary of Clopas and Mary Magdalene' – though he admits that he can cite no other instances of the use of 'sister' for 'sister-in-law'.

He then suggests that the father of James and Joses died and that Joseph took his sister Mary and her sons into his own home, and adopted the two boys, thus making them foster-brothers to Jesus. 'Honesty compels us to admit', he says, that to use 'brother' for 'close relative' 'stretches its meaning to breaking point',[4] but he suggests with some reason that to use 'brother' for 'foster-brother' would be natural. The third 'brother', Simon, he identifies with the Simeon son of Clopas mentioned by Hegesippus, thus making Simon a cousin of Jesus. The fourth 'brother', Judas, he believes to have been related to Jesus in some way we do not know, but not to have been a blood-brother. He sees no reason to think that Simon or Judas were adopted or that the term 'brother' was properly applied to them. In the context it is the opponents of Jesus in Nazareth who lump together the foster-brothers and other male relatives and call them 'his brothers', and they lump together his female relatives and call them 'all his sisters'. McHugh regards with favour a remark of Jerome, which suggests that so many could not all have been blood-brothers and sisters. Jerome called them 'a team of four brothers and a heap of sisters' and said 'we don't say "all" unless we're talking about a crowd.'[5] (But it should be noted, that 'all' need in fact be no more than three, and there is nothing improbable about a family of eight or more children in the ancient world.)

This is an honest and ingenious attempt to find a new solution to the problem of reconciling the dogma of perpetual virginity with the New Testament data. But the theory is based on some large unsubstantial guesses backed by flimsy argument. It requires not only that 'brother' be used commonly and exclusively of foster-brothers and various other relations, it requires that 'sister' be used of 'sister-in-law'. It also requires that the women at a distance and the women at the cross be sharply distinguished, in spite of the fact that even on McHugh's theory two Marys are common to both groups.

In addition, the argument starts from a false premise in its insistence that the James and Joses mentioned in different contexts must be the same people. We have seen already that in the case of James, this is unlikely. Jesus' brother James was one of those who 'did not believe in him', whereas James, son of Alphaeus, was an apostle, who should probably be identified with James the younger. Furthermore, on a natural reading of the text, the ordinary reader would take it that the James and Joses of the resurrection narratives were plainly sons of another Mary, so that the evangelists would have foreseen no reason for their readers to get them confused. Not only is there no need to equate them, such equation can only lead to confusion. Indeed it readily leads to a muddle of Marys, so that some scholars[6] are even advocating an appearance of Jesus to his mother in spite of the fact that for many centuries the New Testament and early Christian tradition had been gleaned meticulously in search of any scrap of information which might honour the Blessed Virgin, without finding any trace of an appearance to her after the resurrection, such as was granted to 'the other Mary'.

OBJECTION TO THE HELVIDIAN VIEW

There is one formidable objection to the view we have taken of the brothers of Jesus and the sons of Clopas. Is not the existence of two families having mothers of the same name, and having three (or even, according to some, four) boys of the same name in a similar (perhaps identical) order, a coincidence too great to be credible? At first glance the odds against it look tremendous, and this is undoubtedly a consideration which has driven many to try to identify the families. Yet, on deeper reflection, it is not difficult to believe. We are dealing with two families of great piety, steeped in the history and promises of the Old Testament. There were current at the time certain names of immense popularity: Simon, Joseph, Judas, John, James (that is, Jacob). Jesus (Joshua) was also rather popular, but in view of the special circumstances in which Joseph's son was given his name, it would have been surprising if Clopas had made use of it. In a smaller measure the same might have applied to John, the God-given name of the Baptist. In any case Johanan, in spite of its general popularity, was neither a patriarch nor a man of distinction in the Old Testament, and might well not therefore have had so great appeal to such parents. We are left then with four names, all of which in such homes were more likely to be chosen than any others.

Matthew and Mark do not say that they are giving the brothers of Jesus in order of birth, but they both place James and Joses first, so it is reasonable to assume that it is a chronological order. Similarly, on the only occasion where the two sons of Clopas are mentioned together, the order is James, Joses. This would mean that Joseph and Clopas (and, incidentally, Zebedee) started with the rather obvious choice of Jacob, the progenitor of the nation. They then went on to Joseph, the most distinguished and admirable of the patriarchs, as a natural second choice. We do not know the order after this, but in any case between Simeon and Judah there would have been little to choose. Simeon, on the one hand, was in fact the most popular patriarchal name; Judah, on the other, was the name of Joseph's and Clopas's tribe and it was the tribe that carried the royal line. Thus, while it is remarkable that the two homes showed such a similar pattern, it is certainly not an incredibly improbable coincidence.

Indeed, *it might not have been a coincidence at all* – who knows what friendly discussions and rivalries there may have been between these closely related families? A mere impression of improbability is no just ground for abandoning conclusions which have come from a careful piecing together of the details of the text in as natural a way as possible. Rather we should see here positive evidence of the closeness of the two families.

THE MOTHER AND BROTHERS IN THE GOSPEL STORY

Although the mother and brothers of Jesus play a small part in the story it seems desirable to fill in what is known about them, partly to reinforce what has already been said about the danger of confusing the family of Mary the mother of Jesus with that of Mary the wife of Clopas, and partly to provide background to the appearance of Jesus to James.

The stories of Jesus' birth and childhood to some extent support what has been said about the brothers. For instance, it is difficult to find a place for the crowd of step-children required by the theory of Epiphanius in the story of Jesus' birth at Bethlehem and in the subsequent flight to Egypt. It is also difficult to imagine that the story of Jesus getting lost at the age of twelve is the story of an only child, as required by the theory of Jerome. Luke tells us that his parents used to go to Jerusalem year by year for the passover.[7] It was not obligatory for the women to attend the feast, but Josephus refers to one particular passover where 'all the people ran together out of the villages to the city, and celebrated the festival having purified themselves, with their wives and children, according to the law.'[8] He seems to regard the presence of women and children as normal. With her much child-bearing and large family Mary probably could not always go, but doubtless it was usually possible to make arrangements for the care of the children. Some would be left in Nazareth with the older women and some would go to Jerusalem with their parents. On this particular occasion it is not surprising that when they set off for home Joseph and Mary, preoccupied with the smaller children, felt no concern that they had not actually seen the responsible lad Jesus in the caravan. But it is hard to believe that parents of an only child would have travelled a whole day before becoming concerned about his absence.

We have very little direct record of the doings of the brothers, nearly everything has to be pieced together from incidental scraps of information given us by the different evangelists. If these scraps of information are arranged in what appears to be the chronological order they make up a coherent story. Indeed they seem to provide a remarkable series of undesigned coincidences, as the narrative switches from John to Matthew, to Luke, to Matthew, to Mark, to John, and back to Mark again.

THE FAMILY MOVES FROM NAZARETH TO CAPERNAUM

The silence of all the evangelists regarding Joseph seems to indicate that he had died before Jesus began his work.[9] Mary, however, seems to have continued to live in Nazareth until about the time that Jesus began his full-scale Galilean ministry. John tells us how on his first return to Galilee from Judea, Jesus 'went down to Capernaum, with his mother and his brothers and his disciples and stayed there for a few days.'[10] (Mary's sister Salome lived at Capernaum, as of course did John himself, when he was not in Jerusalem.) John goes on immediately to tell of Jesus' first clash with the authorities in Jerusalem, and then shortly after he records how Jesus on his second return to Galilee, 'testified that a prophet has no honour in his own country.'[11] Is John perhaps hinting that Jesus had foreseen what was coming and that he and his mother had reconnoitred the possibility of moving to Capernaum?

Then Matthew (without mentioning his mother or brothers) tells of the actual move. Jesus 'withdrew into Galilee; and leaving Nazareth he went and dwelt in Capernaum by the sea.'[12] This was in preparation for his major campaign in Galilee. Then Luke tells us how, after he had made a name for himself in Capernaum, he visited his old home town, how he preached in the synagogue and how they tried to throw him over the cliff.[13] The parallel account in Matthew (and Mark similarly) adds the fascinating detail that the people of Nazareth said: 'Is not his mother called Mary? And are not his brothers James and Joseph and Simon and Judas? *And are not all his sisters with us?*'[14] Clearly Mary and her sons are well known in the town, but are no longer residents there, whereas the daughters, presumably married to Nazareth men, are still living there.

Jesus was head of the household in the new home in Capernaum, where his mother and his (seemingly) unmarried brothers now lived. Though he often travelled, he was not continuously itinerating, and his home was still his base. Matthew and Mark tell us of a number of occasions when he was at home,[15] living in the closest touch with his mother and brothers. John shows that his brothers were right at hand as the Feast of Tabernacles approached and were eager to discuss with him the question of whether to go up to Jerusalem or not.[16] But at that time they did not believe in him and even his mother did not wholly understand him. Mark again tells us how on one occasion when he was preaching to those who had crowded round the house, his 'people' – in the context apparently his mother and brothers – came out to restrain him, saying that he was off his head.[17]

JAMES THE JUST

There can be no doubt that Joseph and Mary had trained their family in the highest standards of godliness, which was later to show itself in the awesome reputation for prayerfulness which James earned as head of the church in Jerusalem. Hegesippus tells us: 'he was in the habit of entering the temple alone, and was often found upon his bended knees, and interceding for the forgiveness of the people; so that his knees became as hard as camels' ... And, indeed, on account of his exceeding great piety, he was called the Just.'[18] It could well be that the unbelief of James and the other brothers (like that of the Pharisees) fastened partly on the seeming laxity of Jesus with regard to the law – with his touching of lepers and dead bodies and his sabbath healings – and partly on the seeming extravagance of his claims. So though it is perhaps unlikely that Jesus suffered outright and sustained opposition in his home, yet he endured all the rubs of an uncomprehending family, so much so that he could specify not only country and his kin, but 'his own house' as not giving him honour.[19]

Right up to the time of the crucifixion there is no indication that his brothers really believed in him. At the news of his arrest they must have been as scared as the apostles were, and they were certainly not at the cross to experience the cruel shame of hearing Jesus commit his mother to John's care. Mary, we have suggested, had come to stay in the house of her sister Salome for the passover. One would expect her family to have observed the passover there with her. If they did, they would have been struck with claustrophobic terror when, just after cock-crow, John and Peter brought them news of Jesus' arrest and of the presence of his captors so near them in the city. They, with no faith in Jesus to sustain them, would, with even more reason than the nine apostles at Bethany, have thought only of escape from the city – which perhaps they effected at first light on Friday morning.

It is impossible to say how long Mary continued to live in John's care. 'From that hour the disciple took her to his own home' could mean that she stayed with him for the rest of her life (as some traditions say), but it would probably be wiser to infer something much more modest. All that the text demands or even suggests is that in the early stages of the crucifixion, soon after the soldiers had cast lots for his tunic, Jesus, wishing to spare his mother the sight of continuing hours of agony, committed her to John. He at once took her away to his home. He saw her through the appalling crisis, but by the time of the ascension she appears to have been reunited with her family.[20]

By that time the brothers had come to believe. James had had a private meeting with Jesus too sacred for telling some time after the great commissioning on the Galilean mountain, when quite possibly all the brothers had mingled there inconspicuously with the crowd. James (like Peter and like Paul) was no doubt one of those who came to love much because he had been forgiven much. Though he had lived so close to Jesus all his life, he had disbelieved him and at the end had not stood by him. But he was to become leader of the church in Jerusalem itself, and was to write of himself as 'a slave of the Lord Jesus Christ.'[21]

NOTES

INTRODUCTION: pages 9–12

1. P.W. Schmiedel, *Encyclopaedia Biblica*, col. 4041; H. Alford, *The Greek Testament*, (Cambridge, 1874; 1st ed. 1849) I 302; P. Gardner-Smith, *The Narratives of the Resurrection* (London, 1926) 60; E. Brunner, *Dogmatics* II (London, 1952) 369; A.M. Ramsey, *The Resurrection of Christ* (London, 1946) 67, 61; P. Benoit, *The Passion and Resurrection of Jesus Christ* (London, 1969) 254; C.F. Evans, *Resurrection and the N.T.* (London, 1970) 3; W. Marxsen, *The Resurrection of Jesus of Nazareth* (London, 1970) 45. (D.M. Beegle, *Scripture, Tradition and Infallibility* (Grand Rapids, 1973) 61 concurs with Marxsen that the biblical passages dealing with the resurrection swarm with difficulties, some details of which cannot be harmonized.); N. Perrin, *The Resurrection Narratives* (London, 1977) 5; J.K. Elliott, 'The First Easter', *History Today* 29 (Ap. 79) 215; ed. I.H. Marshall, *N.T. Interpretation* (Exeter, 1977) 138.
2. G.W.H. Lampe, *God as Spirit* (Clarendon Press, Oxford, 1977) 158: 'Jesus' bones ... cannot be supposed to be elsewhere than in Palestine. That question is of little importance.' J.A.T. Robinson, *But that I can't believe!'* (Collins, London, 1967) 39: 'Precisely what happened to the body we shall never know ... even if the corpse was somewhere around ... it was as nothing to his friends any longer ... For the truth of the Resurrection is a *present experience*.' C.F. Evans, *Resurrection and the NT* (SCM, London, 1970) 41–131. These ninety

pages of form critical analysis of the resurrection tradition seem to lead to the conclusion that there is hopeless contradiction.

Chapter 1: SETTING THE SCENE: pages 13–21

1. Josephus, *Wars* 5: 142–146. The sketch map follows roughly the outline suggested by J. Wilkinson, *Jerusalem as Jesus knew it* (Thames and Hudson, London, 1978) 64. Other authorities draw the north walls differently, e.g. K.M. Kenyon, *Digging up Jerusalem* (Benn, London, 1974) 224; M. Avi-Yonah, *Jerusalem Revealed* (ed. Y. Yadin, Yale, New Haven, 1976) 10. But the differences do not affect the argument of this book.
2. 2 Chron. 33:14; Neh. 3:3; 13:16; Zech. 1:10. It will be observed that in Nehemiah's day fish was brought from Tyre, twenty miles further from Jerusalem than Capernaum. The Mishnah shows that fish was imported from Spain (*Machshirin* 6.3.)
3. See chap. 4, p. 47
4. Matt. 26:17–19; Mark 14:12–16; Luke 22:7–13.
5. p. 35
6. p. 38
7. Acts 1:15, and see chapter 4, page 47
8. See J.E. Hanauer, *Walks In and Around Jerusalem*, 2nd ed. (Church Missions to Jews, London, 1926) 138; L. Farmer, *We Saw the Holy City* (Epworth, London, 1953) 53; R. Brownrigg, *The Twelve Apostles* (Weidenfeld and Nicolson, London, 1974) 89.
9. The precise location and extent of Bethphage is uncertain, but its approximate position must be as shown on the map.
10. K.M. Kenyon, *Jerusalem: Excavating 3,000 Years of History* (Thames and Hudson, London, 1967) 146 154.
11. C. Kopp, *The Holy Places of the Gospels* (Nelson, London, 1963) 382 n 32.
12. J. Wilkinson, *Jerusalem as Jesus Knew It* (Thames and Hudson, London, 1978) 146.
13. G. Cornfeld, *Archaeology of the Bible Book by Book* (Black, London, 1977) 274.
14. The fanciful extremes to which Gordon went can be seen in Wilkinson 198f.
15. I. Wilson, *The Turin Shroud* (Gollancz, London, 1978) 43.
16. J.P. Kane, 'The Tomb where Jesus lay – Evidence from material Remains' (Tyndale Biblical Archaeology Lecture, 1972: MS in Tyndale House Library, Cambridge); *Illustrated Bible Dictionary* (IVP, Leicester, 1980) I 214.
17. Bede, *Ecclesiastical History of England*, Bk V ch 16.

Chapter 2: MARY MAGDALENE: pages 22–33

1. 'The twelve were with him, and also some women who had been healed of evil spirits and infirmities: Mary, called Magdalene, from whom seven demons had gone out, and Joanna, the wife of Chuza, Herod's steward, and Susanna, and many others, who provided for them out of their means.' (Luke 8:1–3)
2. If the complex argument is to be followed the relevant passages should be studied: Luke 7:36–50; Matt. 26:6–13; Mark 14:3–9; John 12:1–8.
3. John 11.
4. At least since the time of Gregory the Great (say from AD 600) the general opinion in the West was that the 'sinner', Mary of Bethany and Mary Magdalene were one and the same person. The Greek church, however, celebrates three separate feasts. The Fathers differed on the point. For a full account, see U. Holzmeister, 'Die Magdalenfrage in der kirchlichen Überlieferung' *Z.f. kath. Theol.* 46 (1922) 402–422, 556–584.
5. One notable example of the maximum doubt approach is the principle of dissimilarity, much used as a criterion to establish the authenticity of supposed sayings of Jesus. This principle says that any element in the teaching of Jesus which is not to be found in either contemporary Judaism or in early Christianity may be regarded as authentic. Sayings which pass this test (which are naturally few and far between) may perhaps claim some extra validation, but it is quite ridiculous to write off sayings which have parallels in Judaism or in the early Church as unauthentic, for Jesus was undoubtedly born in Judaism and he inspired the Church. A sounder approach is to ask the question, Was the primitive catholic Church justified in its belief that the four evangelists were truthful and well informed men, who were attempting to recount the significant facts? If the historian comes to the conclusion that they were, he is then justified in accepting *all* that they say, until at any point error can be proved beyond reasonable doubt.
6. A. O'Rahilly, *The Family at Bethany* (Cork Univ. Press, Oxford (Blackwell 1949) 182. And this list is certainly not exhaustive.
7. J. Jeremias, *The Parables of Jesus* (SCM, London, 1954) 10lf. says: 'It was the greatest disgrace for a married woman to unbind her hair in the presence of men.' 'According to Tos. Sota 5, 9; j. Gitt. 9, 50d it was a reason for divorce.'
8. Matt. 6:17; Luke 7:44, 46.
9. John 11:5.
10. Luke 10:38–42.

11. John 11:17–36.
12. Matt. 26:10–13; John 12:7. Some MSS read 'she has kept' rather than the RSV 'let her keep'.
13. A. Edersheim, *Life and Times of Jesus the Messiah* I 571 describes Magdala and gives references to the Jewish authorities cited.
14. It has been suggested that Lazarus' whole family had moved from Magdala to Bethany and that Mary got her name, as might be expected, because it was her native place, not because it was the place of her notoriety; this would account also for Jesus having friends in far-away Bethany. Though this is possible, it would be remarkable to find Mary living this sort of life in Magdala if her respectable home was there, and it would be remarkable too if the family had happened to move house during the short period between the closing stages of the Galilean ministry and the events of Luke 10:38ff. and John 11. Further, as there is nothing stereotyped about the familiar names which stick to people as a means of identification – e.g. Thomas the Twin, James the Younger, Mary of Clopas, Joseph of Arimathea – the alliterative Mary Magdalene once used would not have been easily dislodged. As to friends in Bethany, Jesus doubtless made a number of new friends in the Jerusalem area on his various visits to the capital.
15. See chapter 4, p. 45 and 147 n.6
16. Mark 14:9.
17. Luke 11:24–29.
18. A. O'Rahilly, *The Family at Bethany* 191.
19. Reuben 2:2; 3:3–6. If, as is probable, this is a Jewish work, its date at the latest must be the first century AD.
20. Matt. 26:7; Mark 14:3; Luke 7:37; 20:38.
21. There are only two passages in the gospels where the word 'prostitute' is used: Matt. 21:31f; Luke 15:30.
22. Even before the crucifixion 'the chief priests planned to put Lazarus to death' (John 12:10).

Chapter 3: THE OTHER ACTORS: pages 34–42

1. See Matt. 27:56, 61; 28:1; Mark 15:40, 47; 16:1; Luke 24:10; John 19:25.
2. Some have argued that 'his mother's sister' and 'Mary the wife of Clopas' are in apposition, thus equating the two. But it is unlikely (to put it mildly) that the Virgin Mary had a sister also called Mary.
3. Matt. 4:13, and see Appendix III p. 137
4. It is interesting that the Fourth Gospel never mentions John himself or his mother or his brother by name. This suggests self-effacingness rather than arrogance.

5. Matt. 20:21; Mark 10:37.
6. In spite of this there have been a number of attempts in recent years to find an appearance to the Lord's mother in the gospels, see Appendix III note 6 page 160.
7. John 19:27.
8. James, the brother of Jesus, for instance, who became head of the Jerusalem church, became known by the respectful title of 'James the Just'. There was a famous rabbi of the early second century AD known as 'Samuel the Little,' (i.e. 'younger').
9. Matt. 10:3f; Mark: 3:18; Luke 6:15f; Acts 1:13.
10. There have been sharp differences of opinion among good authorities on the equation Alphaeus = Clopas. To take two extremes, P.W. Schmiedel (*Encyclopaedia Biblica*, 'Clopas') says: 'Philologically the names are distinct.' A. Edersheim, *Life and Times of Jesus the Messiah* II, 603, n.1 says 'Alphaeus and Clopas are the same name.' The upshot of the argument seems to be a negative one: there are not enough examples of the transliterated names in Greek and Semitic forms to justify a denial of their possible identification. Positive evidence of their identity as one person in the gospels would of course affect the philological argument.
11. In the Syriac (the language nearest to the Aramaic of Palestine) all versions render Clopas at John 19:25 by Cleopas. They do not, however, translate Clopas and Alphaeus by the same name.
12. Eusebius, *Ecclesiastical History* III 11; cf. IV 22. He goes on to record Simeon's martyrdom, how at a great age he remained steadfast under torture (III 32).
13. Edersheim argued further that the two apostles, Simon the Zealot and 'Judas of James' were also sons of Clopas and Mary. Simon the Zealot, he believed, was the Simeon referred to by Hegesippus and Judas of James was *brother* of James the younger. E.J. Goodspeed went further still and contended that Matthew was son of this same Alphaeus (see Mark 2:14), probably by a former wife. This would mean that 'the other Mary' had three sons in Bethany and Clopas four. The arguments for these positions are by no means negligible, but it is unnecessary to pursue their complexities here, for even if they proved convincing, no new principle would be added to our understanding; it would merely underline the interest of Clopas and Mary in Bethany. (See further A. Edersheim *Life and Times* II 602f; E.J. Goodspeed, *Matthew Apostle and Evangelist* (Philadelphia, 1959) 6; J.W. Wenham, 'The Relatives of Jesus' *Evangelical Quarterly* 47 (1975) 6ff.)
14. Luke 8:3; 24:10.
15. See H.W. Hoehner, *Herod Antipas* (CUP, Cambridge, 1972 Zondervan, Grand Rapids, 1980) 303f.

16. Two questions have been raised with regard to Chuza which might undermine our belief that Joanna resided at the Hasmonean palace. Josephus (*Antiquities* 18:5) tells us that the first wife of Herod Antipas was a Nabatean princess, a pagan, whom he divorced in order to marry the infamous woman who procured John the Baptist's death. Now Chuza is a Nabatean name (see Bauer-Arndt-Gingrich *Lexicon*.) which suggests that Chuza gained his position at Herod's court through the princess's influence and it was presumably while there that he married Joanna, a Jewess. The princess, on learning that Herod intended to divorce her, escaped to her father King Aretas, who eventually went to war with Herod. The first question is, when did the war take place? It is usually dated AD 36, but the account in Josephus (though not forbidding it) does not suggest a long interval after the divorce. If war was threatening Chuza could hardly have remained a member of Herod's court. So there is a possibility that Chuza might no longer have been a member of Herod's court at the time of Jesus' death, and therefore that Joanna would not have been resident at the palace.

Secondly, it has been questioned whether Chuza (if alive) would have allowed his wife to itinerate with a travelling preacher, and it has been suggested that Joanna gained her independence through widowhood. It is certainly possible that 'wife' in Luke 8:3 could be used of 'widow', but it is less natural to take the word in this way. Furthermore, Chuza himself (like Manaen (Acts 13:1) and the court official of John 4:46) may have been a sympathiser of Jesus and therefore willing that his wife should help the cause. Living at court would mean that she was not needed as a houswife, but it would certainly have been remarkable if her husband had allowed her to leave him for extended periods. In either case – if Chuza had fled or if he had died – Joanna would probably have lost her place at court and therefore would not have resided at the palace.

There are, then, a number of possibilities which might negate the presumption that we know Joanna's whereabouts. But it is important to notice that this particular location is not necessary to the harmonization. The narratives would still fit together if she had stayed with some other member of the upper classes in Jerusalem.

17. John 18:15; 19:27.
18. Eusebius, *Ecclesiastical History* III 31; V 24.
19. Luke 1:5, 36.
20. A. Edersheim, *The Temple, its Ministry and Services* (London, 1874) chap 7 argues that the author of the Fourth Gospel and of the Book of Revelation has an intimate knowledge of the minutiae of temple procedure.
21. R. Brownrigg, *The Twelve Apostles* (Weidenfeld and Nicholson,

London, 1974) 85, 87f. Brownrigg also makes the following interesting remarks: 'It is not unlikely that the brothers of Bethsaida and the sons of Zebedee were thus linked in a partnership involving the packing, transport, distribution and even sale of their catch. They constituted a cooperative that might well have employed most of the other members of the twelve.' This startling possibility is to some extent confirmed by the use of the terms *metochoi* and *koinōnoi* in Luke 5:7–10, which shows that the two pairs of brothers were in some sense 'partners' who were working together, and by the account of the seven who went fishing in John 21:2, which suggests that others of the disciples beside the four chief apostles were fishermen. To sustain a fish business in Jerusalem, an arduous three days journey from Capernaum, would have required continuous coming and going of a number of men. Perhaps it was in the course of these journeys that members of the cooperative first came under the spell of John the Baptist preaching beside the Jordan crossing, as is so vividly portrayed in John 1, where Peter, Andrew, Philip and Nathanael are all mentioned by name.

Brownrigg then proceeds: 'Unlike Peter and Andrew, however, James and John had a close familial link both with Jesus and even with John the Baptist ... The significance of family relationship in Jewish thinking and its influence on the foundation and progress of the Christian movement has not yet been fully grasped. The fact that the first leader of the Christian Church in Jerusalem was not one of the apostles ... but James "the brother of the Lord" is a remarkable indication of what a family affair the beginning of Christianity was.' Our researches, as far as they go, fully bear this out. There is evident need for the whole matter to be investigated at greater depth. It is intriguing to note (see Appendix III p. 137) that Jesus and his mother and his four brothers moved to Capernaum at about the time when the cooperative lost four able-bodied workers. Could the brothers have taken their place?

22. E. Hennecke, *N.T. Apocrypha* Vol. 1 (Lutterworth, London, 1963) 152.
23. Nonnus, author of a poetic paraphrase of the fourth gospel, who died c. 431, appears, however, by his wording at this point, to think that John was known to the high priest through his fishing business (See J.H. Bernard, International Critical Commentary, *The Gospel according to St. John* Vol. 2 (T & T Clark, Edinburgh, 1928) 593 n 3.)

Chapter 4: THE FIVE WRITERS: pages 43–54
 1. ed. B. Orchard and T.R.W. Longstaff, *J.J. Griesbach: Synoptic*

and Text-Critical Studies, 1776–1976 (Cambridge, 1978) 53.
2. Matt. 26:56.
3. John 18:15, 16; cf. Matt. 26:58; Mark 14:54; Luke 22:54.
4. John 19:27.
5. John 20:3.
6. Mark 11:11, 12, 19, 20, 27; 13:3; 14:3, 16.

7. Mark 14:26, 32.
8. W.R. Farmer, *The Last Twelve Verses of Mark* (CUP Cambridge 1974). It is impossible to summarise this careful and balanced reinvestigation of the subject here. It has an importance far beyond the question of the ending of Mark, for it inevitably raises doubts about the current theory of N.T. textual criticism. It therefore deserves thorough and open-minded study. It was critically reviewed by J.N. Birdsall in *Journal of Theological Studies* 26:1 (April 1975) 151–160. Farmer has directly replied to Birdsall in *Occasional Notes on Some Points of Interest in N.T. Studies* (Bridwell Library, Perkins School of Theology, S.M.U. Dallas, Texas 75275, 1980) pp. 14–20.
I am bound to say that I find the arguments in favour of authenticity stronger than those against. Some brief comments may be in order. Perhaps the strongest argument against the originality of this section is the feeling experienced by many that it does not quite fit what has gone before. For instance, verse 7 raises an expectation of an appearance in Galilee, which is not fulfilled. There is, however, no rule which forbids a writer alluding to an incident which he does not intend to refer to directly.
Again, Mary Magdalene seems to be reintroduced in verse 9, almost as though she had not been mentioned before. The movement of Mark's thought could well be something like this: hearing the angel's announcement of the resurrection, which issued in trembling and astonishment, was indeed a tremendous thing, but it was as nothing compared with the privilege of seeing Jesus for the first time; this appearance was not to all the women, but to one specially favoured woman – the one who had been so marvellously delivered from seven demons. So Mark carefully detaches Mary Magdalene from the other two.
The change in subject from 'they' to 'he' between verses 8 and 9 presents no difficulty. It might have been more elegant if Mark had written 'when *Jesus* rose early', but verses 6 and 7 are so full of Jesus that there is no possibility of mistaking what is meant, and the slightly breathless effect which is produced fits the occasion. Indeed the absence of 'Jesus' in verse 9 creates a difficulty for the view that this section was composed independently, whether as an

addendum to the gospel or for some other purpose. That someone in a new composition should start with 'he', and proceed for ten verses before saying who the 'he' was, is at least as difficult as the view that Mark changed subject at this point.

When Alec McCowen gave his solo recitation of St. Mark's Gospel in a London theatre and later on television on Good Friday 1979, he connected verses 8 and 9 without any sense of inconcinnity. The feeling that the last twelve verses do not quite fit, is partly the effect of conditioning. When N.T. students in the course of a long training have always thought of this section as a non-Markan appendix they automatically read the chapter as if it had two independent sections. It takes effort to see and feel it as a unity.

The argument from style is also often regarded as a very strong one. B.M. Metzger, for instance, says: 'The vocabulary and style of verses 9–20 are non-Markan' (*A Textual Commentary on the Greek N.T.* United Bible Societies, 1971, p. 125). This matter was examined in great detail long ago by J.W. Burgon in his still valuable *The Last Twelve Verses of the Gospel according to S. Mark* (Oxford, 1871) 136–190. He examined twenty-seven instances of phraseology which were held to be suspiciously unMarkan. Of these he concluded that fourteen were nugatory and that thirteen were more or less clearly Markan. In addition he cited fourteen other examples which favoured Markan authorship. Farmer (*Last Twelve Verses* 79–103) in a fresh verse-by-verse examination has concluded that one verse favours non-Markan authorship, six are neutral and five favour Mark.

One final objection to the authenticity of the last twelve verses should be noted. It is commonly said that they look very much like an anthology culled from the other gospels. It is true that there is a parallel to John in verse 9a and parallels to Luke in 9b, 12, 13a, 14a and 19 (according to most MSS), but the parallels show little verbal identity. If, as we argued on pages 120f., 16:15 – 20 is not to be equated with Matthew's commissioning, all the rest of the material is peculiar to Mark. This hardly looks like an anthology. If it was really later than all four gospels it is a strangely incomplete summary of what they say.

9. Mark 14:51f. 'Young man' is used approximately for the age 24–40.
See *neaniskos*, Arndt-Gingrich *Greek-English Lexicon of N.T.*
10. Mark 14:15; Luke 22:12.
11. Luke 24:33.
12. Acts 1:13–15.
13. Acts 2:41.

14. Acts 12:12.
15. John 18:2; Luke 22:39.
16. The scene on the Mount of Olives at Passover time has been likened to a pop musical festival with pilgrims encamped in cheerful chaos on every available bit of land. It would only be possible for someone with inside knowledge to direct the authorities to the right spot if they wished to find somebody. But it seems that Jesus and the twelve were not precisely in this exposed position either in Bethany or in the Garden of Gethsemane. They were not entirely open to public view day and night. It is probable that in Bethany they slept in the home(s) of friends, and that in Gethsemane they retired behind high walls. It is true that Gethsemane is described in vague terms by Matthew (26:36) and Mark (14:32) as *chōrion*, a place or a piece of land, and by Luke (22:40) as *ho topos*, the place. John (18:1–4), however, makes clear that it was a *kēpos*, a garden, *into* which he entered and *out* of which he emerged. If, as seems likely (p. 17), it was a valuable olive-orchard, high walls and a strong gate would have been necessary.
17. John 18:2f.
18. Mark 14:28; 16:7.
19. Colossians 4:14.
20. Luke 13:31; 23:6–12. Luke's account of the visit of the women to the tomb is less emotionally charged than the other three accounts, which befits the report of one who was not of the innermost circle. Another source of information about Herod's affairs may have been Manaen, 'a member of the court of Herod the tetrarch' (Acts 13:1). He was a leader of the church in Antioch, of which Luke was probably a member for some time (see R. Glover ' "Luke the Antiochene" and Acts', *N.T. Studies* 11, 97–106).
21. I in fact believe that the internal evidence agrees with the external testimony. B.F. Westcott set out the argument with beautiful lucidity in his *Commentary on St. John's Gospel* published in 1880. He narrowed the possibilities, showing by means of a series of concentric circles that the author was a Jew, a Jew of Palestine, an eyewitness, an apostle, John. Westcott's view was contested by some and ignored by others, but in the light of modern knowledge (especially that derived from the Dead Sea scrolls) it is now sounder than ever. Leon Morris in *Studies in the Fourth Gospel* (Paternoster, Exeter; Eerdmans, Grand Rapids, 1969, 139–292) has two excellent chapters reviewing how the argument has fared since Westcott's day. That the author was an eyewitness and that that eyewitness was John allows of no doubt in my mind, but for the purposes of this book we shall only assume that the author

made use of the apostle's recollections. For modern attempts to identify 'the disciple whom Jesus loved' with someone other than John the apostle, see G.R. Osborne, 'John 21: Test Case for History and Redaction in the Resurrection Narratives' ed. R.T. France and D. Wenham, *Gospel Perspectives* II (JSOT, Sheffield, 1981) 300f.

22. P. Gardner-Smith's influential book *St. John and the Synoptic Gospels* (Cambridge, 1938) demonstrated to the satisfaction of most readers that John shows no unmistakable signs of having used the Synoptic gospels. This can only mean one of two things. Either, the evangelist (not knowing the other gospels) chanced to write a gospel which never recorded any of the great number of deeds and sayings which they record (or, where he coincided with them in subject, always treated it differently) – which is hard to believe. Or (which is surely right), he purposely selected from his vast resources of knowledge such material as would *supplement* the other three gospels.

23. That the apostolic message was history and not mere story is emphasised in 1 John 1:1–3; Acts 10:41. There are of course those who argue that Paul's theology is incompatible with Luke's. That the two men were of a very different cast of mind is undoubted, but that their beliefs were mutually contradictory is *prima facie* unlikely. Both would almost certainly have been shocked at the suggestion.

24. The accounts are not independent in so much that the resurrection had been the subject of public teaching continuously since the day of Pentecost, and much of what is included in the various gospels was common knowledge. Also (in my view) the later writers knew what their predecessors had set down, but in the resurrection narratives none of them is actually dependent upon an earlier gospel, or can properly be called an adaptation of one of its predecessors. See further my article 'Synoptic Independence and the Origin of Luke's Travel Narrative' *N.T. Studies* 27:4 (July 1981) 507–515.

25. John 21:25; Acts 1:3.

26. I am indebted to the Rev. R.T. Beckwith for the following note: 'Siphre Deuteronomy 190 is the oldest work which disqualifies women from acting as witnesses, and it does so on the rather curious grounds that witnesses are referred to in the Old Testament in the masculine. However, the rabbinical lists of persons disqualified to give testimony do not normally include women, and it is clear from three passages in the Mishnah (Yebamoth 16:7; Ketuboth 2:5; Eduyoth 3:6) that women were allowed to give evidence

on matters within their knowledge if there was no male witness available. Applying this to the resurrection appearances, it would mean that Mary Magdalene was on rabbinical principles entitled to give witness to an appearance of Christ which was made only to her or to her and other women, but it is also intelligible that in listing numbers of resurrection appearances Paul should have concentrated on those made to men. This does not, of course, mean that he was himself unwilling to accept the witness of women in such cases, but that some of his readers might have been.'

27. It is important to note the limitation of the argument from silence. The fact that not even a hint is given of some historical happening is not of course a decisive argument against its occurrence.

28. A careful review of the critical debate surrounding this whole subject may be found in W.L. Craig, 'The Empty Tomb of Jesus', ed. R.T. France and D. Wenham, *Gospel Perspectives* II (JSOT, Sheffield, 1981) 173–200.

29. Acts 2:29ff; 13:36f.

Chapter 5: GOOD FRIDAY: pages 55–67

1. See J.W. Wenham, *Christ and the Bible*, chap. 2, especially pp. 54f.
2. John 10:24.
3. John 1:41.
4. Matt. 16:13–20; Mark 8:27–33.
5. Isaiah 53; Zechariah 13. See R.T. France, *Jesus and the Old Testament* (Tyndale, London, 1971) 103ff.
6. Zechariah 9:9.
7. Matt. 26:28. I assume throughout this book that the passover lambs were killed on the Thursday and eaten that evening as all the Synoptists seem clearly to assert, e.g. Luke 22:7 – 15. John 18:28, however, seems to contradict this, which has led to various attempts to reinterpret the Synoptists in the light of a supposedly different Johannine chronology (see I.H. Marshall, *Last Supper and Lord's Supper* (Paternoster, Exeter, 1980) chap. 3). There is evidence that the term passover was popularly used for the whole period of passover and the days of unleavened bread that followed, and it seems best to take John's 'eat the passover' in the sense of 'eat the meal that fell on that day of the passover festival', that is, the *Hagiga*. The judgment of Edersheim on this still seems sound (*Life and Times of Jesus the Messiah* (Longmans Green, London, 1883) Bk 5 ch 14.
8. John 17.
9. Matt. 26:31f.
10. John 18:1–11.

11. Mark 14:62. Mark evidently gives Peter's version of events. Peter (and Mark) interpret the more literal and enigmatic words 'You said' (which Matt. 26:64 preserves and which Luke 22:70 gives in the form 'You say that I am') as an affirmation. The words of Jesus that follow: 'You will see the Son of Man seated at the right hand of Power, and coming on the clouds of heaven' and Caiaphas' rent clothes bear out the correctness of Mark's interpretation. Jesus had spoken blasphemy worthy of death.

    The type of expression used by Matthew occurs a number of times in the gospels and it always seems to make the best sense to take it as a polite affirmative, as does the New International Version. In reply to Judas: "Surely not I, Rabbi?" Jesus answered, "Yes, it is you." (Matt. 26:25). Before Pilate: "Are you the king of the Jews?" "Yes, it is as you say." (Matt. 27:11; Mark 15:2; Luke 23:3) "You are right in saying I am a king." (John 18:37). There is no reason to think that Matthew, Luke and John are toning down Mark's affirmation of Messiahship.

12. Mark 15:25,33.
13. John 19:25–27.
14. Luke 23:49.
15. Matt. 27:54; Mark 15:39. It is difficult to know how much content there was in this utterance by a pagan soldier. It could be translated, 'Truly, this man was a son of God.' and it might mean, as Luke suggests, that the centurion recognised him as an impressively good man. Luke says that *he glorified God* and said, Truly this man was righteous. This surely means more than the RSV translation, 'Certainly this man was innocent!' (23:47) Matthew and Mark were evidently struck by the form of words 'God's son' coming from a heathen centurion, and Luke too conveys the impression that the centurion regarded the righteousness of this man as having an awesome God-given quality.
16. J.J. Blunt in 1847 wrote a book *Undesigned Coincidences in the Writings both of the Old and New Testament* (Murray, London) which went through many editions. He developed an idea expounded by Paley (*Horae Paulinae*) showing how frequently one passage (e.g. in Paul) unwittingly confirms and illuminates another (e.g. in Acts).
17. John 7:5.
18. Acts 1:14.
19. Mark 15:42. John 19:42. The repeated reference to the 'day of Preparation' (with a capital P) (see also 19:14 and 19:31) is liable to raise unnecessary questions. 'Day of Preparation' simply means Friday and *Sabbaton* means Saturday (in Modern Greek *Paraskeue* and *Sabbato*). If Preparation is spelt with a capital, so should

sabbath be in verse 31. But of course the Jewish day began and ended at nightfall, so the Sabbath began on Friday evening.

20. For the medical aspects of this hideous death, see I. Wilson, *The Turin Shroud* (Gollancz, London, 1978) 26, 28.

21. A. Edersheim, *The Temple, its Ministry and Services* (R.T.S., London, 1874) 222.

22. John alone mentions the garden, which makes congruous this little touch in Matthew and Mark which describes the two Marys as 'sitting opposite the tomb' during the burial.

23. John may well have been present on the occasion when Nicodemus came to Jesus by night (John 3:2). Of the likely possible rendez-vous for this famous meeting, Gethsemane (where the sound of wind blowing in the olive trees would be heard) is an attractive conjecture. But in the ordinary way, except at the great festivals when the city boundaries were extended to include the Mount of Olives within a 'greater Jerusalem', one would expect the city gates to be shut after dark, making a meeting outside the walls difficult, if not impossible. Of homes within the city to which Nicodemus could come expecting to find Jesus, that of John is the most likely.

24. John 11:44.

Chapter 6: SATURDAY: pages 68–75

1. p. 49f.

2. Luke 23:56b and 24:1 contain the particles *men … de*. This probably means that we should attach the last sentence of chapter 23 firmly to the sentence that follows and make it the first sentence of the next paragraph. This would mean that the time of the preparation of the spices is not actually stated and that it could without inaccuracy refer to something done on Saturday evening after their purchase. Nonetheless the impression on first reading is that the preparation preceded the sabbath.

3. See A. Edersheim, *Life and Times of Jesus the Messiah* (London, 1883) I 566; II 358.

4. T.R.W. Longstaff, in his article 'The Women at the Tomb: Matthew 28:1 Re-examined' *N.T. Studies* 27:2 (Jan. 1981) 277 ff. suggests that the women 'went to see the sepulchre' because it was a well known practice that 'friends or relatives often watched at the tomb in case the apparently dead person would revive.' This, he suggests, was the final visit on the third day to confirm his death and it turned out dramatically to be the visit which proclaimed his resurrection. Though possible, it seems better to allow Mark and Luke to interpret Matthew and to see the visit as undertaken for the purpose of anointing the body. Longstaff's theory would

require a number of earlier visits and of these (either accomplished or frustrated) the gospels give no hint.

5. F. Morison, *Who Moved the Stone?* (Faber & Faber, London, 1930) 47ff.
6. Matt. 27:51. According to *The Gospel of the Nazaraeans* (written in the first half of the second century) 'the lintel of the temple of wondrous size collapsed' at that time. Although not a very reliable source of information, *The Gospel of the Nazaraeans* may preserve a genuine reminiscence here. See E. Hennecke, *N.T. Apocrypha* (Lutterworth, London, 1963) I 150, 153.
7. *The Gospel of Peter* should probably be dated about AD 150 or possibly even earlier. See E. Hennecke, *N.T. Apocrypha* I. 179 ff.
8. Mark 8:31; 9:31; 10:34 with parallels in Matthew and Luke.
9. Mark 14:58.
10. John 19:19–22.
11. A. Edersheim, *Life and Times of Jesus the Messiah* (London, 1883), Bk. V Ch. 12.
12. John 18:12. This need not have been more than a detachment from his cohort.
13. Matt. 27:19.
14. Luke 13:1.

Chapter 7: EARLY ON EASTER SUNDAY MORNING: pages 76–89

1. John 12:29.
2. It is probably right to take Matthew's 'Don't *you* be afraid' as emphatic. Though the allusion would at the time have been lost on the women (who did not know about the guard), it was meaningful both to the angel and to Matthew's readers and would in due course have been meaningful to the women themselves.
3. Generally in subordinate clauses, but sometimes also with the main verb, e.g. Mt. 14:3; Mk. 8:14; Lk. 8:27b.
4. W.E. Brown, 'The First Day of the Week' *Scripture* 7 (1955) 46f.
5. Frank Morison (*Who Moved the Stone?* chap. 15) was immensely impressed by Jerome's quotation of a fragment of *The Gospel according to the Hebrews*, which was regarded by J.B. Lightfoot as 'one of the earliest and most respectable of the apocryphal narratives' (*Galatians* p. 274), which says that the Lord gave 'the linen cloth unto the servant of the priest.' On this M.R. James comments: 'This is a famous passage. One interesting clause is apt to escape notice, about the giving of the shroud to the servant of the (high) priest, which implies that the priests must have been apprised of the resurrection as soon as the apostles. Was the servant of the priest Malchus? Presumably the servant was at the sepul-

chre: if so, it was being guarded by the Jews as well as the Roman soldiers (as in the Gospel of Peter).' (*Apocryphal NT*, Oxford, 1924, 4) This fragment is too dubious to bear any weight, but there is nothing improbable about Malchus having been a member of the temple guard which was on duty both at Gethsemane and in Joseph's garden.

6. The story is not altogether absurd. Even though the sleeping guards would not have seen who stole the body, it would be a sensible inference to suspect Jesus' followers.
7. Justin Martyr, *Dialogue with Trypho* (ANCL) 108. And see 'Justin Martyr' *Oxford Dictionary of the Christian Church*.
8. Judges 9:33; Psalm 104:22.
9. E.F.F. Bishop, *Jesus of Palestine* (Lutterworth, London, 1955), 312.
10. The difference has been exaggerated in RSV by its omission on quite inadequate grounds of Luke 24:6a: 'He is not here, but has risen.' RSV follows some Western texts at this point.
11. The two-winged cherubim and six-winged seraphim are scarcely angels.
12. See Bauer-Arndt-Gingrich: *ephistēmi*: 'often with the connotation of suddenness.'
13. In this instance, 'Come' has little sense of motion, cf. Matt. 21:38: 'Come, let us kill him.'
14. Philippians 2:12.

Chapter 8: THE FIRST APPEARANCES: pages 90–102

1. H. Latham, *The Risen Master* (Cambridge, 1901) 40.
2. An elaborate attempt has been made by A. Feuillet to interpret John's account in terms of grave-cloths collapsed by withdrawal of the body. He argues that Peter saw the linen cloths lying flat and the cloth which had been on his head, not lying flat like the other linen cloths, but on the contrary rolled up in the same place where Jesus' head had been and pushing up enough to be visible under the cloth which enveloped it. ('La découverte du tombeau vide en Jean 20. 3–10.' *Esprit et Vie*, 1977, pp. 252–266; 273–284; reprinted *Hokhma* 7 (1978) 1–45.) The discussion is scholarly but it does not carry conviction as a natural reading of the Greek. Nor does it seem plausible as an account of what Peter might have seen, when it is remembered (a) that the cave with its low entrance would have been rather dark, and (b) that the large quantity of spices would have impaired the flatness of the shroud and made it difficult to discern what was underneath it.

Feuillet's interpretation appears to be influenced by a desire to make it conform to data from the Turin shroud. I am not altogether sceptical about this relic, but it is important that the exegesis of the passage should be considered in its own right before external considerations are introduced into the discussion. When radio-carbon dating has shown the shroud to belong to the first century then will be time enough to bring it into the debate.

3. The plural *autous, hautous* or *heautous* is necessitated by the plurality of disciples and need not imply a plurality of homes. The repetition of *pros* in verse 2: 'to Simon Peter and to the other disciple' has also been taken to imply that they lodged separately. This is not supported by verses 3 and 4 which represents them as going out and running together. Perhaps there is a touch of modesty here. Everyone knows about Peter (John is saying), but it was to me too she came; Peter ran to the tomb and I did too.

4. The artists are probably right who suggest that Mary flung herself at Jesus' feet. We are not actually told how she clung to him, but Matthew records how women going from the tomb 'took hold of his feet' (28:9). The Mary at Bethany had also sat at his feet (Luke 10:39) and fallen at his feet (John 11:32).

5. The two uses are well represented in Mt. 10:2: 'The names of the twelve apostles are ...' and Mt. 28:19 (where the verb is used) 'make disciples of all nations'. Of course in the majority of cases the 'disciples' about whom Matthew writes are of the twelve, but it is an inclusive term which in wider contexts cannot be confined to this exclusive group. The remarkable expression 'my brethren' is also used by Jesus when speaking to Mary Magdalene (John 20:17).

6. K. Bornhäuser, *The Death and Resurrection of Jesus Christ* (E.T., Bangalore, 1958) Excursus 2 on 'Galilee', App. 17.

7. Matt. 26:30–32; Mark 14:28; Mark 16:7.

8. Some have thought this unnamed disciple might be the wife of Cleopas/Clopas, but according to Matthew 'the other Mary' (that is, Mary wife of Clopas) had already seen Jesus that day and it seems unlikely that she would not have recognized him. Another suggestion is that it might have been Clopas' son Simeon, who (according to Eusebius, *EH* III 11) became bishop of Jerusalem in AD 61 in succession to James. But if so, it is perhaps surprising that Luke should omit the name of an outstanding man who was destined for this distinguished office. The same objection applies to P. Benoit's suggestion (*Passion and Resurrection of Jesus Christ* p. 275) that it may have been Philip the evangelist who figures so prominently in Acts 8 (see also 6:5; 21:8). For the suggestion that it might have been Luke himself, see *Trinity Journal* VII (1978) 123f. For *Trinity Journal*, see p. 159 App. I, n.1.

9. C.S. Lewis, *Christian Reflections* (Bles, London, 1967) 155.
10. C. Kopp, *The Holy Places of the Gospels* (Nelson, Edinburgh, 1963) 396 ff. defends Amwas.
11. K. Bornhäuser, *The Death and Resurrection of Jesus Christ* (E.T., Bangalore, 1958) 219. P. Benoit, *The Passion and Resurrection of Jesus Christ* (Herder & Herder, New York; Darton, Longman & Todd, London, 1969) 276. There is an interesting parallel in *Joseph and Asenath* (a Jewish work probably of the first century AD) where in chapter 9 Joseph is invited to stay the night at the end of what chapters 3 and 10 show to have been the midday meal.

Chapter 9: LATER THAT DAY AND THE SUNDAY FOLLOWING: pages 103–109

1. In verse 41 Jesus says, 'Have you anything here to eat?' This implies 'Have you anything for *me* to eat?' but it does not actually say that they were having a meal at the time. As they were in a borrowed room, the readiness of their response rather suggests so. Mark 16:14 makes explicit what is already implicit in Luke: 'He appeared ... as they sat at table.'
2. The view of G.W. Trompf ('The First Resurrection Appearance and the Ending of Mark's Gospel' (*N.T. Studies* 18, 327) that the ending was adopted in the interests of harmony could hardly be further from the truth. At first sight it introduces a flat contradiction.
3. James and the other brothers of the Lord may provide marginal exceptions. We do not know precisely when they turned from unbelief to faith. In the case of James it was prior to Ascension Day. They may have turned on seeing Jesus or it may have been earlier through the testimony of friends and relations. For examples of disciples not quick to believe, see Matt. 28:17b; Mark 16:12,14; Luke 24:25,41; John 20:15, 25b, 27.
4. John 11:16; 14:5.
5. The traditions concerning Thomas are carefully considered by C.B. Firth, *An Introduction to Indian Church History*, 3rd ed. (Christian Literature Society, Madras, 1976) ch. 1.

Chapter 10: IN GALILEE: pages 110–117

1. R.W. Funk, *A Greek Grammar of the NT* (Cambridge and Chicago, 1961) 131. cf. N. Turner, *A Grammar of NT Greek III* (T. and T. Clark, Edinburgh, 1963) 37: 'It usually marks a change of subject'.
2. 'Brethren' *may* imply that only men were summoned. There is in

fact no evidence of appearances to women after Easter Day, but neither the use of the masculine word nor the argument from silence about the women can be regarded as decisive.

3. Acts 1:8; Matthew 4:15.
4. Acts 12:17; 15:13; 21:18; Gal. 1:19; 2:9,12.
5. Acts 1:14.
6. James 1:1. James, the Lord's brother, has traditionally been regarded as the author of the epistle, but in modern times this tradition has been widely discarded. In the English speaking world, however, a steady succession of scholars has continued to uphold it, e.g. A. Plummer (1891), J.B. Mayor (1892), F.J.A. Hort (1909), G.H. Rendall (1927), A.T. Cadoux (1944), A. Ross (1954), R.V.G. Tasker (1956), C.L. Mitton (1966), J.A. Motyer (1970), J.B. Adamson (1976), R. Longenecker (1975) and P.H. Davids (1982).
7. Galatians 1:18f.

Chapter 11: FAREWELL: pages 118–125

1. This may be inferred from general probability (see the discussion of John Mark's house in chapter 4) and from the fact that Luke does not change the setting between 24:33 and 24:49.
2. In the United Bible Societies' *Greek N.T.* (3rd ed.) paragraphs begin with *kai* at 14:3, 10, 12, 22, 27, 32, 43, 51, 53, 66; 15:1, 21, 33, 42; 16:1.
3. It is immaterial whether 'forty' is to be taken as an exact figure or as an approximate one. As there were seven weeks between Easter and Pentecost and there was a time of waiting between the day of Ascension and Pentecost, during which there was sustained prayer and the election of a new apostle, there is no reason to doubt that 'forty days' is at least a close approximation.

The question may well be asked whether the New Testament has recorded all the 'many' presentations of Jesus alive during the forty days after his passion to which Luke refers. The answer must be that we do not know, though it can be said that the ten recorded appearances provide a satisfying sequence, which makes no obvious call for supplementation. They tend to decrease in frequency, while leading up to commissionings of great significance.

It is interesting to count up the approximate number of known appearances to difference people:

Peter	6
John, James, Nathanael/Bartholomew	5
Thomas and other apostles	4

The inner circle of women	2
Cleopas (the senior man of Jesus' family)	2
The companion of Cleopas	2
James, the Lord's brother	1 or 2
500 brethren	1

The companion of Cleopas seems to stand out as something of an anomaly in this privileged company, which some have seen as an argument for identifying him with Luke the evangelist, who had 'followed all things accurately from the beginning' (Luke 1:3).

4. The question arises, when did Jesus give the command to stay in the city? Although Luke's gospel telescopes a long series of events, this command is put right at the end of Jesus' instructions and immediately before he leads them out towards Bethany. Similarly in Acts the command not to depart from Jerusalem is put after the mention of the appearances during the forty days and immediately before the final exchange which precedes the ascension. It seems best then to place it among the final instructions given in Mark's house before the disciples went out to witness the ascension.

5. He mentions three, if the appearance to Simon is included; four, if the appearances on Easter Day and Ascension Day are separated out.

6. Eric Bishop with his long experience of the country writes: 'Perhaps Luke's mention of the cloud may be a hint that the experience was in the early morning with the mountains suffused with the mists of gentle spring in Palestine... An all-night sitting would not have been too long for a farewell talk on the things pertaining to the Kingdom of God. Then in the early morning haze, with low-lying clouds alike on Olivet and across the purple ranges of Moab, He said "Good-bye."' (E.F.F. Bishop, *Apostles of Palestine* (Lutterworth, London. 1958) 24.

7. E.F.F. Bishop, *Jesus of Palestine* (Lutterworth, London. 1955) 269. The MSS differ – literally "as far as towards" (or "to") Bethany.

8. Acts 26:26.

9. Paul of course carries the story on further, by saying, 'Last of all, as to one untimely born, he appeared also to me.' Paul does not present his own encounter with Jesus as a 'spiritual' experience in contrast to the physical encounters previously recorded, but as continuous with them. As the three accounts in Acts make clear, Paul's meeting with Jesus was no ordinary ground-level meeting, but it was an objective appearance, in which he heard him with his ears and in which his physical eyes seem to have been blinded by the brilliance of the light which shone from the one who spoke to

him. Though this appearance was after the ascension, we have no
means of knowing whether it was more or less physical than the
other appearances. The relation between the physical and the
spiritual in Jesus' resurrection is helpfully discussed by W.L.
Craig, 'The Bodily Resurrection of Jesus' in *Gospel Perspectives*,
Vol. 1 (JSOT, Sheffield, 1980) 47–74, edited by R.T. France and
D. Wenham.

Appendix I: GOSPEL CRITICISM: pages 126–128

1. A short, tentative statement of my own position on the dating and
inter-relation of the gospels will be found in 'Gospel Origins' *Trinity
Journal* VII 2. (Fall, 1978) 1–23. (Published by Trinity Evangelical
Divinity School, Deerfield, Illinois 60015.) The early traditions
about the writing of the gospels are given there (and can of course be
found in almost any introduction to the gospels). In the same journal
(N.S. II 1 (1981)) D. Moo replies to this article and a brief rejoinder
by me follows. See also my article 'Synoptic Independence and the
Origin of Luke's Travel Narrative' in *N.T. Studies* 27.4 (July 81).

Appendix III: THE MOTHER AND BROTHERS OF JESUS: pages
132–139

1. Luke 2:7; Matt. 1:25.
2. Matt. 13:55f; Mark 6:3.
3. J. McHugh, *The Mother of Jesus in the NT* (Darton, Longman and
Todd, London, 1975) 234ff. The best exposition of the view that
the brothers of Jesus were sons of Joseph and Mary is to be found
in J.B. Mayor, *The Epistle of James* (Macmillan, London, 1892)
chap. 1, which unfortunately McHugh did not appear to know.
This was in part a reply to J.B. Lightfoot's advocacy of the
Epiphanian view in *St. Paul's Epistle to the Galatians* (10th ed.
Macmillan, London, 1896) pp. 252ff. Mayor also wrote the article
'The Brethren of the Lord' in *Hastings Dictionary of the Bible*. C.
Harris in the article under the same title in *Dictionary of Christ and
the Gospels* attempted, but not successfully, to answer Mayor.
4. p. 246. There are instances in the O.T. where the Hebrew word for
brother is used loosely to include cousin, which are discussed by
Mayor in *HDB* I 321b. These are rightly ignored by McHugh.
Precedents could be cited from India for the use of 'brother' for
'close relative', but the culture of Palestine is too far removed for
the comparison to be relevant.
5. McHugh (p. 240) cites Jerome, *Adversus Helvidium*. ML 23,200.
6. e.g. G.W. Trompf, 'The First Resurrection Appearance and the
Ending of Mark's Gospel' (*N.T. Studies* 18 (Ap. 72)) 309ff; J.J.

Gunther, 'The Family of Jesus' *Evangelical Quarterly* 46 (Jan. 74)) 31ff. Gunther's article provoked the author's 'The Relatives of Jesus' (*EQ* 47 (Jan. 75) 6ff.) from which some of the material of this section is taken.

7. Luke 2:41.
8. Josephus, *Antiquities* 11.4.8 (11.109f.). He is referring to a passover in the days of Zerubbabel, but it seems to show that he does not regard the presence of women and children as abnormal. J.B. Segal, *The Hebrew Passover from the Earliest Times to AD 70* (OUP, London, 1963) 254, 257f. thinks that Jesus' visit to Jerusalem at the age of twelve was probably his first, but there is no compelling reason why this should have been so.
9. The remark made at Capernaum 'Is not this Jesus, the son of Joseph, whose father and mother we know?' (John 6:42) was concerned to make the point that his descent from human parents was perfectly well known, but it does not necessarily mean that Joseph was well known at Capernaum at that time. It may, however, suggest that because of his relationship with the Zebedee family there were a good many in Capernaum who had actually met him.
10. John 2:12–25.
11. John 4:44.
12. Matt. 4:12f.
13. Luke 4:16–30.
14. Matt. 13:55f; cf. Mark 6:3.
15. Matt. 13:1, 36; 17:25. Mark 2:1; 3:19; 7:17; 9:33. All these references seem to be to Jesus' home in Capernaum, though in any one particular case we cannot be dogmatic. Once it has been established that he had a home there, the references support one another. G.D. Kilpatrick also understands these as references to Jesus' home. *Journal for N.T. Studies* 15 (1982) 3ff.) Recent archaeological finds appear to have discovered Peter's home in Capernaum, which apparently became the meeting place of the church there after the resurrection. His house is mentioned in Matt. 8:14; Mark 1:20; Luke 4:38. What became of Jesus' home we do not know.
16. John 7:1–10.
17. Mark 3:20f., cf. 31ff.
18. Eusebius, *Ecclesiastical History* II 23.
19. Mark 6:4.
20. Acts 1:14.
21. James 1:1. For references to James subsequent to Jesus' appearance to him, see Gal. 1:19; 2:9, 12; Acts 12:17; 15:13; 21:18; Jude 1.

INDEX